JESUS
—HOPE—
of the
NATIONS

Mary Weeks Millard
with Bishop John Rucyahana

Mary Weeks Millard

Zaccmedia

Published by Zaccmedia
www.zaccmedia.com
info@zaccmedia.com

Published January 2015

ISBN: 978-1-909824-70-6

British Library Cataloguing-in-Publication Data
A catalogue record for this book is available from the British Library.

CONTENTS

DEDICATION

I dedicate this to the many friends and family who have shown me Christ's love in action and brought hope into my life; especially Rev. Timothy Alford and his wife, Pansy, who nurtured my early faith in the Lord; Marcelyn Holmes who became a spiritual mother to me; and my two beloved husbands, Philip Weeks and Malcolm Millard, without whose love and support I would not be who I am today.

Mary Weeks Millard

I am dedicating this book to my dear wife Harriet, with whom I experience the grace of God in our ministry, with thanks for her encouragement and support. We extend our gratitude to God for our children's support and fellowship in God's service. We do thank Bishop Amooti for his constant encouragement to share our story.

John Rucyahana

ACKNOWLEDGEMENTS

I wish to thank Bishop John Rucyahana and Harriet for sharing their story with me and trusting me to share it with the wider world. I also would like to thank Christine Kankindi, PA to Bishop John, who spent so much time helping me in so many ways.

My thanks go, too, to my patient husband, Rev. Malcolm Millard, for all his love and encouragement through the months while I have been writing this book.

I am grateful for the support and help of the West Dorset branch of the Association of Christian Writers who have encouraged and prayed for me as I worked on this project.

My grateful thanks, too, to Paul Stanier, who has been willing to publish this book.

FOREWORD

Great title – *Jesus, Hope of the Nations* is an enthusiastic celebration of many people, especially those who are in the process of accepting Jesus Christ as the Saviour and are in fellowship with Him. It is also a unique and different story, with testimonies, showing the grace of God through different people in different places at different times.

Another element is provided by many interesting biographical details of Bishop John Rucyahana and Harriet, inclusive of all the work in which they have been used by God to fulfil His purposes in the world.

I have witnessed how Rucyahana's life has helped many people to follow Jesus Christ and change their lives even as a refugee in a refugee camp in Uganda. His servant heart was demonstrated in his extreme love when he started Mustard Seed Babies' Home in Uganda and Sonrise Primary and Secondary Schools in Musanze, Rwanda.

He promoted evangelism and development among the Rwandan people; he is really the servant of God in different ways through education, health and conflict resolution. Currently he serves as Chairman of the National Unity and Reconciliation Commission.

My prayer is that all readers will be equally blessed by this book and inspired to love others more deeply and bring hope into their lives, in their homes and community at large. So get ready to be comforted and to experience change through reading this book.

The Most Rev. Stanley Ntagali
Archbishop of the Church of Uganda
2014

HOPE

Hope, hope, hope!
What is my life without hope?
I sink down into a black hole of despair
A place of hopelessness.
Yet, Lord, you have promised hope.
You say you have plans for me – (even me!)
To give me hope and a future.
How can that ever be?
Even before my conception you made plans
For my life – a blueprint – to give me hope!

So, in the darkest times
Let me feel your hope lifting my despair
Lifting me into your arms that care
Helping me to dream your dreams once more.

God of all hope – certain hope
Help me to trust you and your plans
Even when I can see no light ahead
Or when those plans make no sense to me.

May hope spring eternal, by your love and grace
Into this heart of mine.
Hope in my darkness – hope in my weakness;
And lead me into the future you have planned.
Ps. 52:8–9
Ps. 71:14
Jer. 29:11

M. Millard

INTRODUCTION

Towards the close of 2011 I was approached about writing the biography of Bishop John Rucyahana, the retired bishop of Shirya Diocese in Rwanda. Since I was visiting the country at that time I had the opportunity to meet him and discuss the proposal, but I must admit to having grave doubts. This was not because he did not have a story to tell the world, but because one book about his life and work, *The Bishop of Rwanda*, had already been published. Was there a need for another one? However, I left the meeting promising to think and pray about the proposal because Bishop John wanted to cover different aspects of his life in this new book.

Almost a year later Bishop John was in London for a few days and asked if I could meet him again and talk about the proposal. I agreed, even though I was still unsure about undertaking the task. I had a long journey from my home to London and sitting in the train I asked the Lord to give me a word of confirmation that I should go ahead with this project. Then a wonderful thing happened! It was almost as if an audible voice spoke to me. There was just one word, 'hope'.

A few hours later Bishop John and I met and discussed exactly what he wanted to express in this new book. Over and over he used one word, 'hope'! This book is to show how God brought hope to a poor refugee lad and then used him to bring hope to thousands of others in similar situations. I travelled home, not only reassured that this book is part of God's purpose, but also that its title should include the word 'hope'. This was the conception of *Jesus, Hope of the Nations*.

So, in January 2013 once again I travelled to Rwanda, a country which I love and have had the privilege of visiting many times over the past twelve years. After completing my other commitments I was free to spend just over a week with Bishop John and his wife Harriet in their home in the town of Musanze (previously known as Ruhengeri). Although now retired from active ministry as the bishop of Shyira, both he and his wife are far from retired from serving the Lord.

If I needed any further convincing that I should help Bishop John with this book, then living with them in their family and seeing them display such love and hope in action certainly dispersed any doubts!

The more we worked together through that week, the more I became aware of how closely love and hope are linked, and how they need to be translated into positive action, and it is that which transforms lives. I was deeply blessed during that week of research and interviews. My prayer is that all my readers will be equally blessed through this book and be inspired to love others more and be enabled to bring hope into their lives, whether in their own community or further afield.

Mary Weeks Millard
Weymouth, Dorset, UK
January 2014

Chapter One

HOPE AFTER FAMINE

The land was recovering from famine. Indeed, in the history of Rwanda, this famine is known as 'The Great Famine'; however, by November 1945 the rains had returned and the normally very fertile ground had once again produced a good harvest. This was enough to bring hope and joy to the family of John Baptiste Kabango and his wife, Verdiana Karwera, but this joy was increased still further when on November 14th a new baby was born into their family. They named their new son John Rucyahana. His birth was such a delight to them, particularly since the twins who had been born before him had both died soon after their birth.

The family lived in the northern region of Rwanda, the beautiful country which is nicknamed by its residents 'The Land of a Thousand Hills' and by the colonials at that time as 'The Little Switzerland of Africa'. Butete, the area of the family home, was situated about 100 km from the capital city of Kigali and at an altitude of 1,850 m, and is a truly beautiful place. It lies under the shadow of the Virunga volcanoes,* where lowland mountain gorillas still roam in the bamboo forests; and to the south of the village there lies the beautiful Lake Burera.

---

* See figure 001, page 153

John's father was a local chief and, as such, highly respected. He also worked for the Belgian colonial administration until he took retirement in 1957. The wage from his employment enabled him both to feed his family and send the children to school. This was something many families struggled to achieve during this period of Rwanda's history.

Rwanda had been colonised first by the Germans in 1894, when it became part of German East Africa, and then after World War One when Germany's colonies were reallocated, it was given to Belgium to govern since they also governed nearby Congo.

These colonial powers had brought, along with their governance, the Roman Catholic faith, and all who worked for them were required to be baptised into this faith, since it had become the state religion. This practice continued even after independence, and the result was that many people called themselves 'Christians' because they had been baptised, but they had no real or living faith in Jesus as their Saviour and Lord. This was true for John's parents at this time. Indeed, John's father was polygamous, as was the common practice in the country. He was living with three wives. After his conversion to the Catholic faith, as was required by the church, he married one of his wives, but continued to support and maintain his other two former wives and their families.

John's mother gave birth to six living children, so he grew up enjoying a rich and happy family life. However, although they were known to their neighbours as 'Christians' John recalls that it was nothing more than a nominal assent to the faith. There was no real belief in or understanding of Jesus as the personal Saviour whom he later came to love and serve, and who transformed his life, bringing him hope and a future.

Around the age of five, John's formal education began in the small, one-roomed mud-brick building of Butete Primary School. About fifty children managed to squeeze into the small room to learn their lessons by rote. The children all walked to school and were barefooted, too, whether it was wet or dry. Because of this John recalls how the children were all prone to catch jiggers, which are small insects that burrow into feet in order to lay their eggs. If the children's feet were not regularly inspected and the offending eggs removed, then they could have such sore feet that walking became almost impossible and, indeed, lameness could result. Life was not easy for the children in those days. They were expected to help with household chores as well as working hard at school. Water needed to be fetched and carried from the lake each day, and it was a long walk to and from Lake Burera, and uphill all the way back to the village. This was quite a feat for small children carrying the water on their heads! Also, living in the foothills of the mountains meant that it was often cold, especially during the rainy seasons.

John proved to be a bright child and a good pupil. He did so well in this small primary school that he was able to miss the 'primary six' year. At the end of each academic year, even to this day, the children are required to pass an end-of-year examination before they can progress into the next class. However, John did so well that he was able at the end of year five to sit and pass the exam intended for year six. The children who passed this exam with good results were then eligible to continue their studies in primary seven and prepare for entrance to senior school. However, the very brightest children in the whole country who gained the best marks in this year six exam were also eligible to be sent to Murunda, a primary seven boarding school situated in a town called Kanaga, in the Western Province.

John was one of the children selected! It was such an exciting, but also a very scary prospect for him to move away from the village he had known all his life and attend this school! He was the first child in his family to achieve this honour, too, so had no-one to tell him what it might be like.

What mixed emotions he experienced as he moved to Murunda School! Along with the excitement was homesickness which he felt as he left his mother, father and siblings. He missed his mother's home cooking, and also the rich, creamy milk which he had enjoyed each day since his father owned a herd of cows! Now he had to get used to basic boarding-school food! The food was *very* basic, too!

John was also in an exciting new learning environment. There were many strange and new ideas to assimilate. Having only lived in a village setting and being by nature a shy, quiet boy, he was challenged to come 'out of his shell' and socialise, making new friends in order to be happy and survive school life. As all the pupils in the school were very bright and therefore potentially future leaders of their country, they were taught to think for themselves and debate issues, rather than just learn by rote. At first John was very quiet in the classroom, but in time he learnt to analyse facts critically, answering the questions in the classroom and forming and giving his own opinions. He became much more confident.

As Bishop John recalled and shared his memories of these early days at school he commented, "You know, God does work in our lives, leading us into situations by His divine intervention. Even then, in primary seven, he was preparing me for leadership!"

John attended Murunda School for just one year, at the end of which he took the entrance examination for senior school. In those days senior school education was available to a very small minority. Even now, many village children are unable to progress beyond primary school. John passed the exam with flying colours and so was enrolled in the senior school at Gisenyi, a town on Lake Kivu, more than 65 km from his home in Butete. Like most schools in that era, it was run by the Catholic Church. The school had a very good reputation for progressive ideas in education, especially in mathematics, science and technology.

Chapter Two

HOPES ARE DIMINISHED

In 1959 as John was preparing to start at senior school, with all the hopes and dreams of becoming an engineer or maybe a medical doctor, the country of Rwanda was thrown into a time of political and social turmoil.

In Rwanda there are three ethnic groupings; the largest is the BaHutu, and then the BaTutsi, and the smallest group are the BaTwa. The BaTwa are similar to the pygmies of the Congo, a group of small people who were traditionally 'hunter-gatherers'. In Rwanda they were skilled at making pots from clay. Normally these groups are referred to as Hutu, Tutsi and Twa. For hundreds of years they had co-existed happily, using the same language and sharing the same culture. During the colonial era it suited the powers in control, for their own political reasons, to upset this harmony. They used propaganda spread through leaflets and the radio to make the Hutu rise against the Tutsi. It was this propaganda which was the seedbed of the genocide which began in 1959 and culminated in the terrible slaughter of around a million Tutsi and moderate Hutu in 1994. In 1959 the Hutu were incited and encouraged to burn the houses of the Tutsi people. Neighbours who had previously been friends; children who had played happily together, fetched water and sat alongside each other at school; all were suddenly taught that they were enemies. The Tutsi were subjected to being called cockroaches or snakes, and the Hutu were told to drive them from their homes. John's parents' home was one of many Tutsi homes in Butete which was looted and then burnt. Mercifully, his parents escaped with their lives, but decided it was no longer safe to remain in Rwanda and they should escape across the border into nearby Zaire (now the Democratic Republic of Congo). This left John with a difficult decision. He had to choose whether to leave the country and travel to Zaire with his parents or go to Gisenyi to the secondary school. It was such a traumatic time for Tutsi families, hunted, fearing for their lives and losing all their property. Many gave up hope and many young people abandoned their education. Their understandable reasoning was, "We will be killed anyway, so why should we bother to go to school?"

For John it was not an easy decision. He had a vision – and that was to become well educated and in time have a good job. He reasoned, "If I give up my vision, that also will be a kind of death for me", so he decided that he would still go to Gisenyi and hold on to his hopes and dreams.

His mother had a very small amount of money, just 600 Rwandan francs. These she pressed into her young son's hand, tears streaming down her face and with no words to say. It was as if she gave all she had to bless her son. Neither of them could know what the future would hold for the rest of the family or for John.

So John made his way to school, walking most of the way to Gisenyi. He felt excited at the prospect of studying in this secondary school, but was also aware of the risks which he faced because of the violence that was spreading through the nation.

Gisenyi is situated at the head of Lake Kivu and is the border town with Goma, DRC. John enrolled at the school, a Catholic boys' school, mostly taught by priests. He met Emmanuel Kolini at the school, a boy who was later destined to become a lifelong friend and colleague in very different circumstances!

At school John was confronted by the complexity of the national politics. School was no refuge for him from the chaos which was sweeping through the whole of Rwanda.

Of course, school did provide the longed-for opportunity to learn new subjects and study hard, but also to play, too. Wednesday afternoons were free for the boys to enjoy themselves, including going for a swim in Lake Kivu, which has a beautiful sandy shoreline. John had learnt to swim in Lake Burera when he was still very young, so along with playing football, this was often his choice of activity. However, boys could just relax and wander around the town. John was able to stay at this school until the end of 1962, but there were many challenges for him as a Tutsi student. The children whose parents had fled the country were constantly hunted down and even being in a school was no certain refuge for them. Wednesday afternoons became a time when they needed to be constantly alert, often hiding in the bushes to escape members of the Hutu population who would have liked to arrest and even kill them.

When the school holidays came around John would endeavour to walk to Uganda to visit his family, for this was where they had eventually settled. How glad he was that he knew the small tracks and paths around Butete from his childhood days. Using these he could make his way safely to the border. The main roads were certainly not a safe route for him to take.

At one time there was a plot hatched by the militant Hutu students in the school to incriminate the Tutsis. At night they planned to tear down the national flag on the school campus and then burn it, and report to the authorities that the Tutsi students had committed this crime. To do such a thing would be a crime having national repercussions. However, one Hutu student friend warned the Tutsis of the plot, so that they were able to guard the flag and when the militants arrived they raised the alarm. The boys were arrested and were in fact expelled from Gisenyi and sent to other schools.

At this time tensions were evident even within the education system. In 1960 there were elections and the Hutu-backed party,

Parmehutu, gained control, and this result increased the wave of ethnic violence which was already widespread. Prejudice against the Tutsi was evident in that very few members of this ethnic group were awarded places in senior schools or higher education establishments, however good their examination results might be. This resulted in a growing anger, fear and frustration among the Tutsi students. The situation became even worse and when the new academic year began in 1963, John, along with other Tutsi students, was no longer allowed to continue in the school.

This meant their education in Rwanda was now finished. They had to leave without ever completing their studies or gaining a final leaving certificate. This was such a blow to John and his friends who had studied hard and had a great thirst for education as well as dreams of going to university and pursuing good careers. Not only did they suffer that great blow, but also their names were on a 'death list'. They knew they had no choice but to walk through the bush to Goma and seek asylum in Zaire. The town of Goma bordered the town of Gisenyi, so it was the easiest route to safety. By God's grace they helped each other to escape from their beloved homeland of Rwanda, using a series of signals as they hid in the bush, and gradually made their way over the border into the town of Goma. They were safe, but at such a cost!

Chapter Three

CRUSHED HOPES IN
THE CONGO

In 1959 when John's family home was burnt down by Hutu militants his parents fled to the Congo and then to the comparative safety of nearby Uganda. John was one of thirteen children, so they had a large family to care and provide for. In Uganda, refugee camps had been very hastily set up to cope with the emergency situation and these were far from ideal places in which to live and try to bring up a family. Because of this, after a short time the family decided to move yet again. This time they crossed the border back into Congo to see if they could obtain a piece of land where they could settle, grow crops and provide for their large family. They felt it was a better option than remaining in Uganda as refugees.

When John was expelled from school in Gisenyi and walked through the border into exile in Congo, at least he was now in the same country as his family and able to have contact with them again.

In the town of Goma John was able to enrol in a technical school, but he stayed there for only one year. He needed to find work in order to support himself and save money so that he could hopefully return to school at a later date. An opportunity arose for him to work at a tea plantation factory, which John gladly took, hoping it might later help him to get a place in an agricultural college. The plantation was situated in very swampy ground which needed to be drained in order to grow good tea. The job which John was given was to measure trenches and drain the land. With his understanding of mathematics John suggested to the Belgian plantation manager, a Mr. Denowell, who was, in fact, married to a Congolese Rwandese woman, that better drainage would be achieved if different angles were used. John's idea worked brilliantly and the manager was very impressed, so much so that he promised to pay for him to attend the College of Agriculture in Bukavu!

For a young man who had lost everything, his heritage and nationality, his dream of one day being a geologist in the Virunga Mountains, and who had been hunted like a wild animal with even less protection than the native wildlife, this news was a lifeline. From being almost totally without hope, the promise of being sponsored at college rekindled a spark of hope within him. Everything was put into place for him to start in 1965 and he was very excited at the prospect. Sadly, he never did get to the college in Bukavu because towards the end of 1964 war broke out in Congo. All Rwandans were ordered to report to detention centres. There were not enough prisons in which to put them, so schools were turned into centres where they were interned in very poor conditions. Indeed, they were treated and kept like cattle. These were places of great cruelty where many of the internees died and many women and girls were raped. It was around this time that John's beloved father, John Baptiste Kabango, died.

At first, after the order to report to the detention centre, one of John's friends hid him in his house, but being locked in day and night was such a terrible experience that he decided it might be a better option to join the many others from his home area who were now in detention. His friend agreed with his decision to leave and John walked to the small nearby jail in order to give himself up. At the jail he found that one of the officials in charge was his Congolese friend, Zachariah Sebiheri. Zachariah at once made him some black tea laced with lots of sugar. Then as friends they sat and talked. The guards thought that John must be Congolese and didn't immediately arrest or beat him. He did, however, enter the detention centre. It was while he was there that John had a vision, giving him some direction and inspiration. He had been very concerned because in the detention centres the girls were constantly at risk of being raped by the guards and soldiers, particularly during the night-time.

In his vision John saw a lot of woven mats under a tree, each one wrapped around a girl. It seemed there were thirty or maybe forty of them, and they slept under the tree, completely protected from the evil intentions of the soldiers. Then, about 5.30am, at first light, they returned to the detention centre for the day.

The vision helped John to see the way forward to help and protect these girls. He realised that with his friend Zachariah's help they could bring the girls to the safety of the tree each night. The vision gave him hope that he might be able to help others in their desperate situation.

Around this time, John's relatives decided once again that they must relocate, leaving the Congo and returning once more to Uganda. They felt this choice was the lesser of two evils. At least there was still peace in Uganda and a measure of protection, even if it meant life in a refugee camp. John was also now thinking that the only option left to him was also to flee to Uganda. His thoughts were crystallised after he was involved in an incident which left him a marked man.

One day, in broad daylight, two armed soldiers grabbed a young girl aged around fourteen or fifteen, with the intention of raping her in front of everyone. Even her stepfather seemed rooted to the spot and unable to move to help her. John was horrified. He could hear the girl's cries of pain and despair and no-one went to her aid. John grabbed a walking stick called an *inkoni* and asked two young men near him to help him save the girl.

John, looking the soldiers in the eye, challenged them to shoot him and promised them a beating to within an inch of their lives, waving the inkoni in their faces. The soldiers cursed and shouted, and one kicked the young girl and told her to run away. It had been a very scary incident and could have resulted in his death, and John knew after that experience he really had no choice but to get out of the detention centre and escape to Uganda. Both the family of the young girl and also the soldiers came from the area near the tea factory where John had worked, so they knew exactly who he was. Before he left the Congo there was one last thing which John needed to do. He went to visit the place where his father had been buried in order to pay his respects; then he began the walk through the bush to Uganda in November 1964.

Chapter Four

THE START OF REAL HOPE

After John had walked across the Rwandan–Ugandan border at Kisoro, he made his way to a reception centre in an Anglican mission at Seseme. Many Rwandan refugees were pouring over the border in a second wave of exodus from the Congo. At the reception centre the refugees were registered and then packed onto trucks like cattle and driven to the large town of Mbarara where they were accommodated in a temporary refugee camp for about a week. After this they were then reloaded onto the trucks and driven north to Bunyoro, a district of North West Uganda, situated close to the river Nile. The refugee camp was called Kwangeli. It was not a nice place to live! For people who had lived in Rwanda and Congo where there are many hills and mountains which keep the temperature down, this area was exceedingly hot. It was also full of malaria-carrying mosquitoes, which bred unhindered around the river Nile. Not only was malaria a real problem for the refugees to face, but also a strange new disease spread, called *buruli*. After infection, boils spread over the patient's body. This was very painful and caused many deaths. The water in the boreholes was infected, too, so that dysentery and cholera spread rapidly. On top of this, the refugees were given maize for food, which was old and not fit to eat. Most of the people from Rwanda had no idea how to cook maize because it wasn't grown in their country, so another cause of sickness and death was food poisoning. John recalls that while he was still a boy in that camp, every day he was called upon to help with the burial of dead people from morning to evening each day; and it was a haunting, harrowing experience.

That refugee camp was a place where no-one had any hope. It was just a place of mere existence. Children had nothing to do and nowhere to go, so hundreds of them loitered around the camp from daybreak to dusk. There was nothing of importance on which to focus the mind – days just drifted by without hope. John, reduced to existing in that camp, felt he could never have hope again after the two huge disappointments in his life, first the expulsion from the school in Gisenyi and secondly, not being able to enrol in the college at Bukavu. It seemed as if all hope, decency, human rights and human dignity had disappeared when he became a refugee. No longer were there any choices – you had no choice where you could live, no choice about the kind of life you could live. Everything was stripped away from you.

One day the Minister of Culture for Uganda came to the Kyangweli refugee camp and addressed the refugees. There were around 10,000 people living there at that time. His message was far from encouraging and very discriminatory. The people had each been given a small plot and had built little mud huts with grass roofs.

"You people," he told them, "you are forbidden to grow bananas or coffee on your plots. You may only grow temporary crops. If the wild pigs come and eat them, then chase them away very carefully. They are Ugandan and have more rights of protection than you who are not Ugandans! You have no rights to protect your crops. They are temporary like you!"

Many years later, when John was living in a town in Uganda called Mukono and studying at the theological college, this same minister was very sick in Mulago hospital, in Kampala. John went to visit him and told him of the Lord's love for him and asked if he could to pray for him. God had taken the refugee whom this government minister had deemed to be of less value than a Ugandan wild pig and given him the grace to forgive the insult and lovingly to pray for him!

In the refugee camp John began to attend the services held in the Anglican church. In his heart was a lot of bitterness, not towards God, but towards the Belgians who had done so much harm to his country and also towards the religion they had brought and the many priests who had complied with the violence against the Tutsis. His old school friend from Gisenyi, Emmanuel Kolini, was also now a refugee in Kinyara and he was attending the church, too.

One thing which deeply concerned both of these young men was the plight of the hundreds of children who roamed around every day. They had absolutely no hope for the future. They had not even had the opportunity to study in school and so have any hope for a better life. They spent their days fighting over trivial things or perhaps leaving the camp and trying to steal from the surrounding villages. Something had to be done for them! At least these two young men knew enough themselves to give them an elementary education. So they started a school in the church building. Emmanuel Kolini was the headmaster and John the other teacher. They used the church building and divided the children into two classes. Emmanuel taught one group, and John the other. The classes sat at opposite ends of the room, trying not to disturb each other It was very rudimentary, but it was a start. Neither teacher owned a watch, so they told the time by the position of the sun and finished school when it was high in the sky! Some of those early pupils have gone on to become high achievers in post-genocide Rwanda. A little hope was being implanted into their lives. There was something they could work for, something they could attain!

For John himself, hope was rekindled about a year after the school started. It was then that he met the Lord.

John had come to the realisation that he had lost even his very self, his sense of personhood, in the refugee camp. He could see no hope or future, when one day Jesus came near and revealed Himself. He had been reading the book of Acts in March 1966 when he saw clearly that in Jesus there was hope – hope for his own life, hope for all the refugees around him – hope for the nations. As John read the book of Acts, he knelt down just where he was, in his khaki shorts and white shirt, confessing his sins, and asked for forgiveness and the sure and certain hope of a new life in Jesus both for the present, his future and eternity.

"I cried alone, and I cried out of my heart to the Lord," he told me, recalling that wonderful day when everything changed for him.

"The following Sunday," John continued to tell me, "I openly spoke to the people in the church. I told them I had confessed my sins and was now depending on the Lord Jesus."

That day marked a change not only in John's personal life, but also in his vision for the children whom he was teaching. Up until then the children had sat on logs in the makeshift classroom and written with sticks in the dust of the mud floor. He had only had a heart of love and his head knowledge to share with them. Now he felt motivated and courageous enough to appeal to the Ugandan church leaders to ask for blackboards and chalk. Soon the school grew to 600 children. John felt compelled in his love for the children to show them that the future belonged to them, not as refugees in a camp, but as Rwandans; however, they had to work for it! In God's redemptive purposes many of these children went on to succeed and become 'top people' in different spheres of life.

John's friend, Emmanuel Kolini, who had also by now become a deeply committed Christian believer, heard God's call to the Anglican ministry. He left the refugee camp and went to train in Burundi, leaving John as the new headmaster. A purpose-built school was being constructed and all was going well when the Ugandan government suddenly decided to transfer everyone in the camp 100 miles away to a new camp at Kyangwali, east of the town of Hoima.

Here everyone had to start their lives all over again. First the land had to be cleared of the trees and bushes, then little houses had to be built. In 1977–8 John finished building a new school in which to teach the children. Many refugees were arriving at Kyangwali from other camps and so there were many, many children.

In this new camp the Christians began to meet regularly together to pray and worship, and from this group a church was planted. It had a thriving youth group made up of many of the schoolchildren, and the Lord used this group to herald a revival both in the camp and also in the surrounding area.

John encouraged the young people as they went out to the nearby villages and preached the gospel to others. They also tried to show the love of Jesus to the families around them in the camp, helping the elderly with chores which were difficult for them, and sharing the little they had with the very poorest of the poor. As hope was growing in these young people, so they were able to show this love to others and bring hope into their lives.

Chapter Five

HOPE COMES TO HARRIET

Rukara is a town not far from the beautiful Lake Muhazi in the eastern province of Rwanda. It was here that Harriet was born in 1954 into a family of fourteen children. Her mother gave birth to three children by her first husband, and then eleven more by her second husband, who was Harriet's father. Very sadly, only four girls survived and Harriet was the second eldest of these. When she was just six years old, the 1959 uprising against the Tutsi people group began. Once again, since the family were Tutsis, they were hounded out of their home and country. Harriet's mother was called Mary and she, together with her three eldest girls, escaped from Rwanda by trekking through the bush and over the border to the safety of Uganda. It was difficult for Mary, since her youngest daughter was still a baby and needed to be carried on her back. It was a hard journey for her to make alone, but Harriet's father was now dead. He had died in 1959 when Harriet's youngest sister was just five days old.

The family went first to a refugee camp in Rukinga. Although Harriet was only a child she recalls the terrible food which they were given to eat, and how so many people died at that time because the food was rotten, but also because the Rwandans just didn't know how to cook the maize meal and make *posho* porridge from it. The conditions were so bad that even very small children, such as herself, went to work for the local Ugandans in order to earn one little banana which they could eat. The elders in that camp were also concerned about the children's welfare and education and started a small school for them. There Harriet and her sisters learnt to write in the dust. The family stayed in this camp for the next four years, but during this time Harriet's mother succumbed to illness. The family were then moved to another camp where her aunt was living, but the conditions there were even worse so in 1964 the family moved yet again, this time to Kinyara camp in Bunyoro. It was such a hot, dry and barren place in which to live. There was no clean water supply and mosquitoes abounded. So many people became sick and died. It seemed as if they just moved from one bad place to an even worse situation!

There was famine at that time in Kenya and many Kikuyu people had also migrated to Bunyoro seeking land to cultivate. They were not refugees and were able to start farms. In time Rwandans from the camps would go to work for them from 5am until 6pm trying to earn a few Ugandan shillings in order to alleviate their poverty.

Harriet's two younger sisters started at the school where John was the teacher. At eleven years of age, and having had almost no education, Harriet was thought too old to join the school and so stayed at home to help her mother. By 1966 the family had procured a little plot of land and Harriet worked in this garden, trying very hard to produce some food for the family to eat. Starvation was like a hungry wolf never far from the door!

Although Harriet's mother was not a Christian, she allowed Harriet to go to the church with her friend who was called Vanessa. This friend was an orphan, weighed down by sadness and anger, and was seeking a way to find healing for her pain. Alongside her friend, Harriet listened week by week to the preaching and teaching. They often discussed the things which they had heard and began to pray together. Forgiveness was a big issue for Harriet to grapple with; there was a lot of bitterness for what had happened to her and her people and their forced exile. She felt as if she was always asking God, "Why? why? why?" At the end of 1966 Harriet asked the Lord to forgive her and cleanse and heal her heart. Publically she stood up and witnessed to her decision to follow the Lord. She knew her prayer had been answered because her heart was filled with a freedom and peace. All the burden of bitterness which she had been carrying for years had been lifted from her.

However, life continued to be hard. Harriet farmed the unproductive land trying to grow food; she cut down long grass in order to put a new thatched roof on the hut, and collected grass to burn in order to drive away the mosquitoes, but she also now had hope in her heart and knew that the Lord was looking after her. Harriet then had a new desire growing in her heart. She longed to be able to read and write and began to teach herself to do so.

Harriet saw John from time to time when she took her younger sisters to the primary school and also at the fellowship meetings in the church. Then, when the Ugandan government decided to move people from the Kinyara camp to a new one at Kyangwali near Hoima in 1967–8, Harriet and her family also relocated to what eventually proved to be a far better place in which to live since the land was more productive, and therefore food became more plentiful.

By this time, Harriet's older sister had married and left home. Harriet was quite content to stay and look after her mother. Indeed, she had no real desire ever to get married. She felt that with the Lord as her Saviour her life was now happy and complete. She also had a fear that if she married, she could be hurt again. She didn't want bitterness and pain back in her life!

Harriet's friend, Vanessa, had also married, and she and her husband towards the end of 1967 invited her to visit them in their home. Here they formally introduced her to John, as is the custom when a young Rwandan man is interested in a young lady. However, Harriet was not interested in this young man! Harriet refused his advances and gave John her reasons for not wanting to proceed with their friendship:

1. She hadn't been to school and felt uneducated, whereas John was a teacher.
2. She had no desire to get married.
3. She told John to seek another girl!

John, not to be daunted by this initial refusal, wrote a letter to Harriet saying he wanted to marry her and could they meet again and talk. A further formal introduction meeting was arranged and Harriet's heart softened to a 'maybe', and she began to pray earnestly about his proposal.

Then, in her mind, Harriet produced another list of reasons why perhaps she should marry this young man:

1. He was a born-again Christian.
2. He wouldn't hurt her.
3. He spoke the truth.
4. She knew his character and testimony from his witness in the church.

So, in the end, Harriet accepted John's proposal and they were married on December 20th 1969.

Harriet and John's marriage has been greatly blessed by the Lord. She has been a wonderful helpmeet for John throughout his entire ministry as well as a homemaker and mother to their five children and, later, three adopted nieces and nephews. In the early days of marriage there were many hardships to endure because there was so little money, but there were no complaints from Harriet. Two weeks into their marriage they moved yet again to a new location and a new post for John.

They were blessed by the birth of Grace, November 8th 1970; Patrick, August 20th 1972; Hope, November 12th 1975; Joy, November 7th 1979; and Andrew, 6th April 1983.

All these children would agree, as Proverbs 31:28 states, "Her children arise and call her blessed; her husband also, and he praises her."

Chapter Six

BRINGING HOPE TO THE IMPOVERISHED PEOPLE OF BUNYORO

It had been the Anglican Church of Uganda which had shepherded and cared for many of the Rwandans who were exiled in their land, bringing hope to them as they preached the gospel of Jesus. This church had, in previous decades, been greatly blessed by the spread of the Rwanda revival into East Africa. The revival was known as the 'Balokole' movement. Now the Ugandan Church had an opportunity to reach out to the Rwandese people, bringing the love of Jesus to the refugees. Bunyoro at that time was part of the Anglican Ruwenzori Diocese, and the Bishop was a very godly man called Yosanani Rwakaikara. He was concerned for and had a deep compassion for his flock. Many children in the area were malnourished, suffering from the diseases of kwashiorkor and marasmus. Kwashiorkor develops when a child is deprived of protein in the diet. The child's body gradually becomes swollen, the hair turns orange, and the skin peels, leaving weeping sores. The condition is not only difficult to treat when advanced, but normally leads to death. Marasmus is a condition where the child is starved of all types of food. The child becomes thinner and thinner and eventually dies. The biochemical changes in the bodies of these children are very difficult to reverse, so treatment is more than just giving them food. To counteract these diseases Bishop Yosanani wanted to start in his diocese a 'Christian Rural Service' (a scheme introduced to Uganda by Bishop Light). This scheme incorporated social development and Christian witness in the villages, enabling people to escape from abject poverty and feed their families and learn about the love of God.

Bishop Rwakaikara needed someone to head up this scheme, and he sensed that John would be exactly the right person for the job. He approached John and asked him if he would be willing to start the scheme in Bunyoro. First, it would mean going to Kabale to train with Bishop Light for eight months as an evangelist for the Christian Rural Service programme.

At first John was not at all sure about this suggestion. It would be very hard to leave the school and the children in the refugee camp. He had spent years developing it to a good standard and giving the young people a hope for their future. However, this new opportunity would give him a chance to move out of the camp and share Jesus with the wider Bunyoro community. Prayerfully, John reached a decision and agreed to take the position. His months of training were both practical and theoretical. When he returned it was to a place called Seseme and no longer as a refugee, but as a missionary. He felt confident, as he came back, that he could be a blessing and bring hope from God to an impoverished society.

The new post gave scope for many activities. John went to visit various centres, including Kisoro and regions even further north, and began to teach the village women how to make nourishing food for their families; how to cultivate vegetables instead of only buying them at the market stalls, and to sell the excess for profit; and how to form clubs where they could help and encourage each other. John's teaching skills were also used as he taught literacy classes to these people.

In the Bunyoro region there was plenty of land available for cultivation, so John worked with two other missionaries who had World Bank funding to set up a co-operative. They worked with school 'drop-outs', trying to inspire them to lead more productive lives. Each young person was given 10 acres of land and a loan to buy stock. Five acres were to be used as a small tea plantation and the other five for general food crops. When the tea began to crop and was sold, then the repayment of the loan would begin. This way, with a small amount of money left to live on, the loan was soon repaid and the young person became an independent farmer. The five acres of food crops also produced enough surplus to enable a further income to be made at the market. Many of these youngsters settled down, married and also came to know the Lord. The practical love and help shown to these people really softened their hearts to the gospel, and their lives took on new meaning and hope. The wider community was helped, too, as John was able to get hold of tractors which enabled much greater yields of maize production. Again, John was able to encourage people to join together and work in co-operatives, harvesting from bigger acreages and hiring trucks to sell the produce in the capital, Kampala. This way the people began to make a good living from selling maize and also red peppers.

The spiritual harvest was blossoming too! Three new parishes were planted and so both the social and spiritual landscape changed. This model of evangelism had a significant impact on John for his future life and ministry, for he saw how taking the gospel out of the pulpit and into the community had the power to transform lives in a holistic way.

It was very exciting when a group of men and women who had been part of the co-operative scheme asked for confirmation. After a wonderful service the bishop commented to John that it was the first time in his career that he had met such a group of young people, filled with the Holy Spirit, who really wanted Jesus to be the very centre of their lives!

For five years John, with Harriet at his side after their marriage, served these communities in Bunyoro. He felt very fulfilled and happy and so was not a little taken aback when the bishop approached him and suggested that he should go to theological college and train for the ordained ministry.

"Why?" was John's response. "People are already getting saved; the youth are very enthusiastically tithing and using this money to organise weekend seminars and conventions. Why do you want me to leave this work and sit at a desk for three years?"

This godly bishop replied with insight, "God is preparing you to minister on a wider scale. If you don't study, then you won't be ready, and some doors will be shut to you if you have no qualifications."

He counselled John to pray about his calling and also to trust the Lord that He was able to use others to continue the work which was now thriving in Bunyoro. So John took the advice and sought the Lord, who confirmed to him that he should obey. So it came to pass that in 1972 he enrolled in Bishop Tucker Theological College in Mukono. It wasn't easy for Harriet and the family. Married quarters were given only for the final year of training, so Harriet had to return to live with her mother in the Kyangwali refugee camp, taking little Grace with her, and awaiting the birth of Patrick. Grace had a nickname: 'Nice'. It had been given to her when she was born and a pastor had asked what her name was. John and Harriet told him that she was called Mbabazi which meant 'grace'. The pastor was convinced that it was a pagan name, but after lengthy explanation that it was indeed, very Christian, his comment was, "That's nice!", and ever after called her Nice!

Patrick was born in August 1972 when Harriet was living with her mother back in the refugee camp. It must have been very hard to return to a refugee camp after living 'normal' lives in Bunyoro and working with John in such a fruitful ministry.

Meanwhile, John needed to hold fast to the conviction he now had, that the Lord wanted him to study at Mukono. Before he left Bunyoro, some of the brethren prophesied that his going would prove to be a disaster, and that he would become spiritually dry from studying theology. However, John had realised that God is the God not only of uneducated people, but also of the educated. The Lord revealed to him that St. Paul was well educated and, because of this, God was able to use him to take the gospel to places where he could not otherwise have gone. This confirmed to him that he was on the right path and he determined to study as hard as he could. First he had to work very hard to improve his English, because he had no school certificate and had come from a French-speaking educational background. John also had to first take a mature student's entrance examination before he could study for his Diploma in Divinity or a degree.

In 1974, John passed his Mature Entrance Exam and graduated. Then on December 8th of that year he was ordained on the shores of Lake Albert by Bishop Yustus Ruhindi, who was the first bishop of the newly formed diocese of Bunyoro-Kitara.

Chapter Seven

HOPE THROUGH THE REIGN
OF TERROR

After John's ordination as a deacon in the Church of Uganda he and Harriet were sent to work in the parish of Kigorobya. The parish was very demoralised because the previous minister had left, having failed to get enough support from the parishioners to pay his meagre salary. If John was not able to turn the situation around within a year, then he was told by the bishop that the parish would be closed. The diocese promised to pay his salary for a year, after which the parish must be able to take responsibility to pay it, if the work was to continue.

So John's ministry began with a huge challenge. He worked very hard preaching the gospel, doing pastoral work in visiting parishioners, outreach and Bible teaching. The people responded and the church grew. In September 1975 the Bishop made a visit to the parish. There were more than 900 men and women waiting for confirmation! It was an amazing visit for him and he stayed three days, visiting all the small churches and meeting the congregations. Wherever he went he was greeted by jubilant believers. The day before the confirmations were due to take place, the Bishop sent for his wife to come and witness the wonderful work which God was doing. At the end of the service the Bishop announced that the parish would not be closed after all, as the congregations were able to support their pastor and also able to build a church building. After that visit, the bishop ordained John as a priest.

In spite of this great encouragement, the ministry still had many struggles. Some of John's parishioners were fishermen who worked down at the lake. In order to evangelise them, because they slept through the day and worked at night, he took to having midnight meetings for them. This was on top of his full daily workload.

There had been a history of poor money management in the parish, with corruption and embezzlement. John proved very unpopular with some of the church members as he organised teams of his staff to collect the tithes and offerings and banked the money, in preparation for purchasing the building materials for the new central parish church. He was determined to set an example of honesty and transparency when it came to the use of money. Submission to the Lord and His Word brought John into conflict with some people who were used to doing and having things their own way. Others, however, were thrilled to serve humbly, and did so with love and excitement.

At the end of John's second year in the parish the untimely death of the archdeacon Kirahwa of Masindi in a car crash shocked the whole Anglican Church in Bunyoro Diocese and was the cause of John being asked to leave his thriving parish. The dean of Hoima Cathedral was sent to Masindi to comfort the congregations there who were grieving for their beloved archdeacon. This left a vacancy on the cathedral staff and, about a year after the crash, John was appointed to this position, even though he was still a very junior pastor. Not only was he fairly newly ordained, but he was still a young man and also, being a Rwandan, he was a 'foreigner', so rather than give him the title of dean, he was designated 'vicar' of Hoima Cathedral.

As such, John did much of the 'grassroots' work of the cathedral. He was very blessed in that he had a godly and wise canon to help him. Canon Florence Njangali had been the very first Bunyoro woman to be ordained. At this time she was probably already in her late sixties. They had regular times of prayer together and she comforted and encouraged the young vicar. Springing out of one of these times came the idea to hold an English service at the cathedral, since in the town there were many people who came from different Ugandan tribes but for whom English was a common language. Of course there were those who objected to this, feeling it would diminish the numbers at the Bunyoro service. John argued that overall it could only add to the numbers of worshippers, not diminish them. In discussion with the canon her only question about such a service was, "Did you hear the idea from men or from God?"

John's response was, "From God."

"Then go right ahead," she counselled. "Don't be afraid or care what men might say!"

So John took her advice. The English service was started, and thrived. It grew within a year to be as large as the Bunyoro service and in two years it had doubled again in size, so much so that it needed another minister. Then Rev. Geoffrey Tibenda was appointed to join the team. In time, from this service a youth group was born, and many young people who joined this were from the Catholic Church as they felt more at home with a liturgy in English. John was concerned. He didn't want to be 'sheep stealing' in a spiritual sense, so he visited the Catholic bishop, Edward Bakaragate, to talk about the situation. The bishop was very encouraging.

"Love and disciple them, but please don't baptize them," was his response.

John stayed in this post at the Hoima cathedral from 1977 to 1980, during which time the congregations not only grew, but were transformed by a new enthusiasm.

All of this was happening at a time of severe social upheaval and unrest, now looked back on as Amin's 'Reign of Terror'.

In 1971 Idi Amin forcibly took the over the country of Uganda, by a military coup, from President Milton Obote. At first, Amin was welcomed as the hero who had freed the people from the oppressive rule of Obote, but this soon changed as people realised they had fallen 'from the frying pan into the fire' and this new regime was equally brutal. Eight years of terror for the people of Uganda ensued. They were eight years of economic disaster, too, as Amin expelled the Asians who ran so many of the businesses and replaced them with his relatives, friends and soldiers, most of whom had no idea of commerce. Food prices soared, while plantations were left to become overgrown and factories disintegrated into rust and rubble. Thousands of people were killed and their bodies thrown into the river Nile at Jinja, Murchison Falls and Bujagali Falls.

Amin was a Muslim and he recruited more and more Nubian Sudanese Muslims to take ruling positions. The Christians in Uganda were marginalised at the very least, and targets for the death squads if they were outspoken about the atrocities which were occurring everywhere. Amin had shot and murdered Archbishop Luwum for daring to speak out against the regime. Then he tried to cover up the murder by staging a road accident. Educated people from all walks of life were targeted for annihilation. Bank managers, Government ministers, university lecturers and many other professional people disappeared, only to be replaced by uneducated soldiers. He strained relationships with the wider world and took the country out of the British Commonwealth, declaring himself the 'Conqueror of the British Empire'. He even made some British people carry him on their shoulders through the capital city, Kampala, in the manner in which chiefs were carried in olden days.

Through these years John was teaching and preaching the truth of the gospel, and so without doubt was a marked man. Terror had seized the whole country. If the Ugandans were terrified, then how much worse it was for the Rwandan refugees! They had no rights and no protection. Some Ugandans decided that the Rwandans were a bad omen for the country and so they became objects of violence and hate in many ways during those terrible years.

In his deluded state of mind, Idi Amin decided to invade Tanzania in 1979. He felt himself to be invincible. When he entered Tanzanian territory it gave the Tanzanian army the opportunity to retaliate and come to the aid of the people of Uganda, resulting in the overthrow of the brutal regime and allowing Dr. Milton Obote to return once again as President of the country. This second term of Obote's rule proved to be even more corrupt and evil than his first term in office. Then there ensued a terrible time for many refugees, especially those living in the Ankole region. They were hunted like animals and their houses burnt down, their land and their cattle confiscated. Some were chased back to Rwanda, where it was still unsafe for them to live. Even in their homeland they were herded into refugee camps again. So for many of the refugees, living in exile was far from being a peaceful, safe experience. They had no way either to repatriate to Rwanda or to take Ugandan nationality. They felt dehumanized physically and psychologically. It was hard for them to be productive in any way, yet they did survive and ultimately flourish even in such hard conditions.

In 1979 in Bunyoro, although the Tanzanian army had liberated most of Uganda from President Amin's reign of terror, his soldiers had retreated to, and still controlled, the area. It was Easter time and the official drum master went to the drum house at the cathedral and, as the custom was, began to drum to celebrate the festival even though it was still night. John was asleep but the noise of the drumming woke him up. He knew that the noise would anger the retreating soldiers and cause trouble. He quickly dressed and in order not to be seen he crawled through the bushes to the cathedral drum house and remonstrated with the drummer. "You must not drum now – it will cause offence to the soldiers; you must stop at once!" he told him. Although the master drummer was drunk he eventually listened to what John was saying and stopped drumming. John was then able to return to his bed. However, after a little while, the drummer changed his mind and returned, beginning to drum again, and once more it woke John and once more he went out to stop him. By this time an irate group of Amin's soldiers had arrived at the cathedral and went storming through the compound. They took revenge by capturing a group of students and some resident pastors who were studying at the Bible College on the Cathedral campus, driving them away on a truck. Some of these men told the angry mob of soldiers that the cathedral vicar, John Rucyahana, was the person responsible for all the activities and services and that included the drumming. Because the students had also told them that John was a foreigner, a Rwandan refugee, as well as being the person responsible for the noise, the soldiers decided to capture him and kill him. The mob of soldiers then drove to John's house and took him away. By now he was already robed for the services. They had a car waiting, ready to take him away to his death. Looking at the group, John recognised one of the soldiers. He was called Ali, and was a guy whom he knew personally. He looked at the mob, then invited them all into the house to have tea and talk. They refused his invitation and asked, accusingly, "Were you rejoicing because Amin fell to the enemy?" John told them truthfully what had happened, and how he had gone twice to stop the drumming.

Then one of the soldiers said, "That man is speaking the truth." He told the others that some of them had gone out when the drumming first started, ready to kill the offenders, but then it stopped and so they went back to the barracks.

John explained that the drummer was known to be a drunkard and, being at that time very much the worse for drink, he had returned to drum again and so he had gone a second time to stop him.

"Then we want to know the name of the man who was drunk!" the soldiers demanded. John knew these soldiers were intent on murder so he negotiated a deal with them that if they found the drummer and he had a 'hangover', then they would not shoot him.

"He didn't know about the fall of Kampala," John explained. "He is just a drummer who calls people to come to the church services."

Just then another pick-up truck arrived, this time with more soldiers. One of these immediately put a gun to John's head while another took a shot at the verger, wounding him. They wanted to kill both John and the verger, but Ali, the soldier known to John, intervened. "Let's check out this story first," he advised.

The angry soldiers listened and so John was made to sit in a truck full of hand grenades and landmines while they drove to the house of the drunk drummer. The soldiers had intended to blow up the cathedral and all the buildings in the compound! Mercifully none of the explosives detonated while John was sitting on top of them on the bumpy road!

When they arrived at the house of the drummer, they found him still suffering from the effects of alcohol. The soldiers arrested the man and started to beat him. Somehow John found the courage to challenge them, reminding them of the deal that they had made with him, promising not to kill him. The mob of soldiers were very angry, but miraculously did stop. A defeated army in retreat is always very dangerous like a cornered wild animal!

Driving back to the cathedral, John had yet another trial to face. A different group of soldiers had been to the cathedral and arrested some church members and were now taking them to a prison. When they saw John they stopped the truck he was in. A soldier jumped out of the first truck and put a gun to John's head. He was about to pull the trigger and kill him when another of the soldiers in the truck with him pushed the gun away and explained that John had been the one to stop the drumming, not start it. So he was reprieved!

Although John was unharmed physically, the insecurity that ensued from knowing yet again that he was a displaced person, disposable, and all he had striven to do in the past years could be taken away from him in an instant, caused him a deep psychological trauma.

After this traumatic incident, the bishop of Bunyoro and Kitara recommended that John went away for a further period of study. So John returned once more to Bishop Tucker Theological College in Mukono, which was affiliated with Makere University, to study for his DipTh (Diploma in Theology). This period of study was for another three years and meant that yet again he would have an enforced separation from Harriet and the family. For Harriet, it meant another return to the refugee camp to stay with her mother from 1981 to 1983.

Chapter Eight

BRINGING HOPE AFTER AMIN'S RULE

After the liberation of Uganda, the country faced many new challenges. Much of the infrastructure and economic situation had to be completely rebuilt and it took a long time before life regained any semblance of normality. One experience which John had demonstrates this powerfully. On one occasion he was on a bus travelling back from Kampala to Hoima, when they arrived at a roadblock and all the passengers were ordered to get out of the vehicle. The soldiers scrutinised the passengers one by one and decided that John bore a resemblance to Museveni, a powerful politician – who eventually became the President after Milton Obote was finally ousted from power for the second time.

"You look like Museveni – maybe you are him in disguise!" they said roughly to John and instantly arrested him. Then they ordered the other passengers to return to the bus.

One woman refused to get on. "This is our pastor," she declared. "We cannot leave without him!" Then some of the other people agreed and climbed off the bus, too. The protest produced an argument which might have become an impasse except that a policeman recognised John and confirmed his identity, so he was allowed to continue on his journey. Maybe there was a slight resemblance, because John was arrested five times during the second regime of Obote, and each time with the accusation of being Museveni in disguise! Uganda continued to be a country where extreme injustice reigned, and the ensuing fight to overthrow the president and restore peace to the country was a very sad and insecure time for many Ugandans.

After John had finished his studies at Bishop Tucker College in Mukono and graduated with his Diploma of Theology, he returned to the diocese of Hoima. He was then appointed as an archdeacon and oversaw a jungle area situated between Masindi and Hoima. The terrain was so difficult that even travelling through it on a bicycle in order to reach the parishes was a great challenge. John had the task of setting up new parishes and sorting out all the administration for them, so he needed to hold meetings in many different places. People were still randomly being arrested and killed, but in spite of that, John had to travel around and continue his work. For a period of time the diocesan secretary went on leave and John had to add his work to the already heavy workload, and become caretaker of the whole diocese. Even so, the mission and growth of the Church expanded in an amazing way through these difficult times. The churches were full for every service, and even though the soldiers were still killing many Christians, they were not deterred from meeting publically together. Even when they had burial services for their murdered members, the soldiers would turn up and shoot over the heads of the mourners in a menacing way. They didn't like the people being buried; they wanted their bodies to rot in the streets or be eaten by dogs and treated as if they had no rights or dignity.

This was a time when many Ugandans decided they must leave their beloved country and go into exile. John and Harriet had to face the challenge of whether they would stay in the country. After all, they were still regarded as refugees – Uganda was not their homeland. Should they apply to be refugees in America or Canada? One of John's brothers had been granted asylum in Canada after almost being killed in Kampala. However, John and Harriet felt, after much prayer, that God was calling them to stay and continue to minister in Uganda. In obedience to the Lord, they not only stayed, but saw the Lord bring an amazing harvest in the diocese.

John was able to train seventy-five lay evangelists, and with this team he preached throughout the area. God worked in such wonderful ways that even the remnant of the East African 'Balokele' revival was revived! Bishop Yosanani gave his permission for large crusades to be held throughout the diocese. In preparation for a Sunday crusade, the team would go to an area the week before and conduct a house-to-house visitation, talking with people and inviting them to the Sunday meeting. Afterwards, follow-up meetings would be arranged for those who had responded to the gospel. Although the country was still in political and economic turmoil, the gospel was spreading like wildfire, bringing hope into people's lives. There was so much joy as people found the wonderful salvation of Jesus for themselves!

John and Harriet forged many deep friendships during this time which survive even today. Friends from Bunyoro still cross the border in order to attend events in Rwanda and encourage their beloved archdeacon and his wife!

It was during this time that John and Harriet's family life changed, too. In 1986 one of John's brothers died, leaving a widow and four children. His widow, Adera, was not strong and she was left with one pre-school little girl, Grace, and two sons and another daughter who were of primary school age. The eldest, Jack, should have been in primary four; but he was already opting out of school and running a bit wild. John and Harriet were very concerned for the family and prayed a lot for them all. Both of them felt that perhaps God wanted them to take this family as their own, but were hesitant to share this with each other. It was a huge commitment for a couple who were struggling to feed and clothe their own children! Finally Harriet spoke out her inner conviction and John agreed that they should take care of the family even though it seemed a crazy idea and they didn't know how they could implement it.

Once they had made the decision to bring the children to their family and enrolled the older children in Bulindi Primary School, little Grace was given some financial support by an African Evangelical Enterprise project in Kibogo. This was a blessing and a great help, for which they were very grateful, but then a real miracle happened!

After some long weeks of prayer about the situation, a visiting team arrived in the area from Florida and they needed an interpreter. An American lady, Janice Kimbroogh, with her husband Bill, came to do this. After they had interpreted the message Harriet took them into the house for coffee, because they looked hungry and thirsty. As they were leaving, this couple gave them an unexpected gift of 600 American dollars, possibly because they had seen all the children running around, and noticed, too, that they were very needy. This gift was the miracle they needed! With it they were able to build a simple house for Adera, John's widowed sister-in-law. So the whole family moved near them and the children went to school, ate at John and Harriet's home, but also were able to see their mother.

It wasn't easy, but God's grace had enabled them to be obedient and take these children into their own family. It gave the children an opportunity to have hope and work for a better future.

One dear friend counselled John and Harriet: "How can you take these four children into your family when you have no means to provide for them, and struggle to care for your own?"

John answered him, "I have brought them here to love them, and those are the only riches I have to give!"

John and Harriet knew that God had directed their decision and that day by day He would help them to manage. These children have all grown up to be useful, educated and productive people.

John reflected that had Harriet and he not listened to the Holy Spirit and obeyed His prompting, they would have blocked God's blessings to the whole family. They had used just 'mustard seed' faith and then saw how the Lord enabled it to grow. They had one rule to which they unfailingly adhered. Even if there were great family needs, church money was *never* to be used to meet them. Church funds must always be used with transparent honesty; about that there would be no compromise. God honoured the stand they adopted on that issue and blessed the love which they poured out on all nine children. Now they have a harvest as they see their children and grandchildren with the seeds of faith growing in them.

In 1987 the Ugandan government offered John Ugandan citizenship* in acknowledgement of his great contribution to Ugandan society in education and social welfare. This was a wonderful miracle, and meant that John was no longer a stateless person! With his citizenship came the automatic right for Harriet and the children to buy citizenship too. Having a Ugandan passport also meant that he could now travel abroad for further study.

The theological college at Mukono had links with the Trinity Episcopal School for Ministry in Pittsburgh, Pennsylvania. The bishop sent John there in order to study for a master's degree, MAR, and he majored in history.

Yet again it meant that he had to leave Harriet and the children and travel on his own. After one year he pleaded with the school's authorities to allow Harriet to come and join him. John was aware that his experiences in the West could alienate him from his beloved wife if she wasn't able to share them with him. There was a strange rule that made it compulsory for the American students to bring their wives to the college, but forbade the Africans from doing the same! Through the kindness of an English friend, Bishop Taylor, who donated a sum of money which he had saved for a holiday, John was able to bring Harriet, Joy and Andrew to America. Harriet wasn't permitted to take any courses but she did experience the American way of life. Further support for her stay was given by some other friends, Drayton and Fairfax. This sacrificial giving blessed the

---

* See figure 004, page 155

family so much! The rest of the children were by now in boarding schools, so they remained in Uganda, spending the school holidays sometimes with relatives, and sometimes with beloved family friends, Zacharia and Stella Kaheru.

It was a great day of celebration in 1990 when John graduated with his MAR from Trinity! He and the family then returned to Uganda, and back to Hoima Diocese to take up their work with fresh vision and enthusiasm.

Chapter Nine

HOPE AT THE MUSTARD SEED BABIES' HOME

For a person to 'live in hope' means that they will not allow their circumstances to define who they are. It means refusing to settle for less than that which God has planned for their lives. How can people who are enslaved by abject poverty and hopelessness be helped to make such decisions? I believe that Bishop John and Harriet would answer, "By showing them practical love – the love of Jesus!"

When the Rucyahana family returned to Uganda from America, they were confronted with a group of people who had absolutely no way of helping themselves. Following the devastating years of the Amin government and then the second Obote administration, the country had been stricken by an HIV/AIDs epidemic. This resulted in many babies being born who were infected with the virus. Babies were being found abandoned and left to die. There was a huge stigma attached to a child who was thought to have been infected with HIV. John and Harriet were horrified to find these little ones dying from neglect and decided they must do something in the Hoima area to help them.

Sometimes, little children who were completely healthy but were the offspring of parents infected with the disease were just abandoned. There was so much ignorance and fear about the disease.

John and Harriet's care and concern for these babies resulted in founding and funding an orphanage which they called 'The Mustard Seed Babies' Home', a refuge for abandoned babies. They recruited a matron called Evas Bitatoho to look after the babies. This lady was a very experienced nurse who also had managerial skills. She had experience of parenting, being a devoted mother of two boys. Most importantly, she was a deeply committed Christian with a loving heart, who would care for the babies as if they were her own.

So the home for these babies was started. Children were rescued from all sorts of terrible circumstances. Some were found on rubbish tips and others even found in the mouths of dogs who roamed the countryside!

From small beginnings this home grew to house around fifty children. Of course, they did not remain as babies for long but grew up to attend local schools, and later some went on to college and university. The ethos and vision of the home was to help the children to achieve their potential, rising from the ashes of poverty to become the stars of society! When they enrolled in school these children would refuse to have themselves recorded as 'orphans' by the school management; they were proud to say they came from 'Mustard Seed Home' and they were not orphans, for they had a Dad, John Rucyahana!

The home went from strength to strength and after only four years was given an award by the Ugandan Government, who ranked it the best baby home in the whole country. Even after John and Harriet left Uganda and returned to Rwanda they continued to love the children and support the home. As time went on, improvements were added. Solar panels were added to the building, a means of utilising the sun for power to heat water etc. A farm was developed where food could be grown, and poultry and cows were kept and bred. This not only provided food for the children, but also they learnt farming and animal husbandry skills. All these things were used to bring transforming hope into their lives.

After John's return to Bunyoro-Kitara Diocese to resume his work as the archdeacon of Bulindi and Kiryadongo, he was appointed by the bishop to serve on the national board of planning and development of the Church of Uganda and continued in this role for several years. It entailed reviewing new policies for the Church for both development and finance. He also served in the Project and Development Department as the chair of the Projects Committee, so all in all he held a very responsible post. All this experience in the area of development was to prove invaluable when John and Harriet later returned to help the devastated country of Rwanda after the genocide.

There was always a deep concern in John's heart to help alleviate poverty. One project which he was able to start was to provide heifers which would give milk and become a source of income to some of the poorest families in Bunyoro.

He longed to see people be able to reach their potential in Christ and help themselves to climb out of the pit of poverty. John's wide experience had taught him that hope did not lie in just handing out aid in various forms to poor people, but in the rebuilding of a healthy self-image which would then enable that person to find the strength within himself to work towards a better future.

The year that John returned from America, there were new hopes among the Rwandan refugees in Uganda that perhaps they could be repatriated. In 1979 the Rwandese Refugee Welfare Foundation had been formed to help victims of injustice after the fall of Idi Amin. In 1980 the name changed to the Rwandese Alliance for National Unity and the ethos also changed as the group became more militant, advocating the return of the exiles to their homeland. Some of the young men from this group helped the Ugandan Minister of Defence, Yoweri Museveni, in his struggle to oust Milton Obote from his second term in power. This group became the core of the Rwandese

Patriotic Front which was the political and military movement that eventually liberated Rwanda in 1994.

The RPF leaders approached the President of Rwanda asking permission to return to their homeland as full citizens. If permission was not granted, they warned that they would repatriate themselves by force.

The President's reply was, "There is no room for you in Rwanda." So an invasion force crossed the border in 1990.

It was against this political backdrop that John was also appointed to be the diocesan Missions Co-coordinator. He organised missions and conventions throughout the Bunyoro area. John was delighted to be involved in outreach and the preaching of the gospel. He led teams which also spread beyond the borders of Uganda and into Rwanda, in spite of the tense political climate there.

In both countries the years of war, oppression and poverty had brought a spiritual hunger into people's hearts. It was thrilling to see people find that hunger satisfied as they came to know Jesus and His salvation.

In January 1995 John organised a three-day convention which was held in Bunyoro. Christians gathered from all over East Africa and even from the United Kingdom. It was to be the climax of John's ministry in Uganda. It proved to be an amazing time when many experienced God's power in a new way in their lives, with wonderful healing and deliverance taking place. Many pastors returned to their churches totally revived by the Holy Spirit and with renewed vision for their ministries.

After this convention, John and Harriet received a request from the Church in Rwanda asking if they would be willing to return to their homeland, in order to help to meet the needs of the people who were trying to recover from the terrible 1994 genocide.

Chapter Ten

HOPE IN THE AFTERMATH OF GENOCIDE

Nelson Mandela once said, "I have discovered the secret that after climbing a great hill, one finds many more hills to climb. I have taken a moment here to rest, to steal a view of the glorious vista that surrounds me, to look back on the distance I have come. But I can rest only for a moment, for with freedom come responsibilities, and I dare not linger, for my long walk is not yet ended."

I am sure that John and Harriet would understand exactly what Nelson Mandela was saying. Having climbed many 'hills' in Uganda, they could take only a moment to rest because new challenges and responsibilities lay ahead. Even though they had come so far, ahead of them lay another difficult and steep path.

Their beloved homeland of Rwanda had been plunged brutally into civil war and genocide in April 1994. Many books have been written to try to explain this terrible event, and many stories of heroism and survival recorded. Although on this one dark day of history in April 1994 a genocide erupted which proved to be the fastest genocide recorded in modern history, behind that evil day lay years of festering social, political and economic problems. The same hatred and persecution of the Tutsi people which had driven John and Harriet from their homes into the safety of Uganda now drove thousands more refugees to pour into Uganda, Burundi, Congo and Tanzania, as well as others who tried to escape further afield to Europe or to North America. Thousands more didn't make it to safety. Within the space of three months around a million people perished, mostly Tutsi, but also moderate Hutu who would not join in the killings or tried to help their Tutsi neighbours to escape.

The RPF was in Rwanda, and occupied the east and parts of the north, engaging with the government soldiers to try to stop the killings and free their countrymen from the terror. As soon as Kigali was liberated and it was possible (though not very safe) to do so, John went to Rwanda to his old 'home' area to see what could be done to help. He decided he could take mission teams from Uganda into that area to preach a message of healing, hope and forgiveness.

John's heart had been burdened and broken as he listened to radio broadcasts and realised that the world had seemingly turned its back on his beloved homeland. Even the United Nations forces fled, leaving the country to its bloody fate! The UN Security Council refused to give their soldiers on the ground a mandate to stop the slaughter.

The rivers in eastern Uganda were polluted by the number of dead bodies which were being swept into them from Rwanda, poisoning the fish and other wildlife. John was aware that some of those dead bodies may have been those of people he knew, friends and family; old people and little children. It was a horrific thought. These thoughts crystallised in his mind: he must return to help Rwanda!

It was from this decision that the idea of taking evangelistic teams over the border came to him. He gathered a group of eleven pastors and in a rented minibus they travelled over the border to see what the country was like. John told the pastors that they needed to understand what had happened, however horrific that was, before they could bring a message from the Lord. It was like Job's friends; they needed to sit and weep and feel some of the depth of pain, in order to earn the right to speak.

In those early days, when the genocide had barely stopped, Rwanda was a pitiful place. Bodies still lay unburied in towns and countryside. Some had been reduced to skeletons by vultures and dogs, others were still rotting in the heat, and the smell of death was everywhere.

Hastily made mass graves also revealed the horror of the event, where body parts were partly sticking out of the ground. Houses had been broken down, burnt and looted. There was wanton destruction. Electric sockets pulled out of the walls; water and electricity supplies purposely damaged; family pets killed. Cattle had been stolen and destroyed. Everywhere was evidence of destruction and devastation, and the land was laid bare.

People who had survived the war were terrified and bore the physical and emotional scars of the torture and rape to which they had been subjected. Parents had been brutally murdered in front of their children; children had witnessed their parents being hacked to death. Even now, many years after the event, the screams of the victims still reverberate in people's minds. Little groups of orphans gathered together to try to form some sort of 'family'. They became known as 'child-headed families'. Could this country ever recover from what had happened?

Because not all of the country had been liberated, the team of pastors stayed at a military camp and was shown around the area by a lady guide. The trauma of what they saw overcame three of the pastors and for several days they were out of their right mind. Even the guide became traumatized at one house they visited which was still full of bodies; there were twenty-six humans and also the remains of the pet dog and cat.

The RPF had needed to supply a guide because many of the roads had been mined by the government forces. The group needed to be guided through roads which had been cleared of mines.

The experience of that visit was horrendous, but necessary. How else could they even begin to understand the evil which had happened? Even today, although the bodies have been reburied in memorial sites throughout the country, it is important for visitors to Rwanda to see these, in order that they can begin to comprehend the scale and sheer satanic brutality of what happened.

John believed that only God could heal his fractured homeland and that Jesus was the only hope for the nation of Rwanda. He also knew that God used patriotic people, however inadequate they felt, to do His work.

After the initial reconnaissance visit, John began to take evangelistic teams from Uganda to Rwanda, to share the only hope there was, the news of Jesus' love and forgiveness. He continued to do this regularly for the next three years, working in particular with church leaders, encouraging them to strengthen themselves in the Lord and minister once more the love of Jesus to their people.

When John received a letter from members of the Shyira Diocese of the Anglican Church in Rwanda in 1997, begging him to return on a permanent basis to the land of his birth, where he was so needed, it was not an easy decision for him and Harriet to make. John committed himself to serious prayer, knowing that he would be going to live in what was effectively in many ways still a war zone. In his prayer times he became more and more convinced that Rwanda needed to hear a new message of hope and that God was appointing him to preach it. God told him clearly that He needed a man, a Rwandan, who had not been part of the violence to preach that message. Then the Lord sent John dreams about how Rwanda could be reconstructed and he knew beyond any doubt that he must answer the call.

When John wrote back to the people from Shyira Diocese who had challenged him to repatriate, he agreed, but had many questions. He needed to know what job he would be required to do and wanted to make it very clear from the outset that he was not going to be involved in church politics. The Anglican Church had been torn apart by divisions from before the genocide. Then John was asked if he would be willing to have his name put forward to be elected as bishop of Shyira. After once again stating that he would not become involved in the church politics, he agreed to the suggestion.

The next step was to inform the Bishop of Bunyoro-Kitara Diocese in Uganda that he would be leaving. It was hard for the bishop to release John into this new work, even though he knew the needs were great. John's work as mission co-coordinator had been so blessed by the Lord, with many thousands of people having been saved. However, he did lovingly release John and Harriet into this new ministry and wrote a wonderful commendation for them.

John and Harriet left the security of their home and position in Hoima and returned to live in Rwanda. Their children were in good schools in Uganda, so they left them there to complete their studies, but arranged for them to return home for the school holidays. Even that was a risky decision as living in Rwanda was still very hazardous. After the genocide officially ended, many militant Hutu fled to the safety of Congo, but from time to time raided the Northern Province where the Rucyahana family relocated, killing, raping and looting. In the whole of the area there were roadblocks and often random killings. The fact that John was a minister of the gospel gave him no protection as this office was no longer held in respect. Too many pastors had abandoned their flocks during the genocide, and respect for ministers of the gospel had disintegrated. The Northern Province had always had a large population of Hutu people, so the infiltrators thought they would be accepted, and it was comparatively easy for them to walk through the bush into Congo and then back to Rwanda without crossing the official border post.

During the genocide about 10% of the population had been killed, and 30% exiled as refugees. Those who remained in Rwanda were severely traumatised and left with a country which had become a wasteland. Even the normally fertile land had become so blood-soaked that the crops were failing. John and Harriet moved into a very challenging situation. However, they went knowing it was a very clear call from God for them to do so.

51

A few months after their return on June 8th 1997, John was consecrated as Bishop of Shyira Diocese, which at that time covered three Rwandan provinces: Ruhengeri (now Musanze), Gisenyi (now Rubavu), and Kibuye (now Karongi).

Chapter Eleven

HOPE FOR THE PRISONER

One inevitable result of events such as the Rwandan genocide is that afterwards the perpetrators must be brought to justice. Thousands of people were arrested and sent to prison. This was necessary for the security of the general population and for justice to be administered. By 1997 around 125,000 men and women were interned in the prisons. Every prison in the country was overcrowded and living conditions in them were appalling. Most of the prisons were old and without adequate facilities. Thousands of the prison population were Hutus who had participated in genocide, but as well as those people there was the normal prison population which would have included all three of the country's ethnic groups. This in itself could bring tensions among the inmates.

In a few prisons the overcrowding was such that there was no room for the prisoners even to lie down on the floor to sleep at night. It resulted in some of them developing such swollen ankles that gangrene developed and amputations needed to be performed in order to save their lives. It was obvious that something had to be done to deal with the problem of overcrowding. To address this the government took the measure of allowing the elderly, juveniles and the sick to be released and this eased the pressure a little. However, it immediately brought into focus a problem for the families of their victims. How should they react? How could reconciliation be achieved? There was no way that Rwanda could survive as a nation unless a way was found whereby people could be reconciled and live together once again in harmony and interdependence.

Prison Fellowship International is a global association of 110 national Prison Fellowship organisations. The groups exist all around the world and have a network of more than 100,000 volunteers who work in local prisons to help the spiritual, moral, social and physical wellbeing of prisoners. They also work with their families, caring for them and helping ex-prisoners to settle back into the community, as well as supporting the victims of crime. The work of this organisation is trans-denominational and has been widely acclaimed throughout the world.

In 1996 Pastor Deo Gratis Gashagaza accepted the post of Director of Prison Fellowship Rwanda. He had also repatriated back to Rwanda after the genocide about the same time as Bishop John, who became the President of the group PFR (Prison Fellowship Rwanda). They began to work together in the prisons to bring hope and encourage justice. In Rwanda the Prison Fellowship embraced a specialist ministry different from many other parts of the world because they had to deal with many people who had participated in genocide.

They first had to gain permission from the government to be permitted to work in the prisons, and this was granted. It was a privilege because no other religious group was offering to do this work immediately after the end of the genocide. There was no financial help available to fund the work; the men were just aware of a calling from God, a great compassion for the prisoners, and a vision that something needed to be done for them.

In agreeing to share this work, Pastor Deo and Bishop John knew they would have to travel vast distances in order to visit all the country's prisons. This in itself was a challenge as vehicles were still being hijacked and passengers murdered as they travelled in certain areas of the country. Even fuel was not always freely available, or spare parts should repairs to vehicles be needed.

As the two men started to meet with prisoners, some of the needs began to be revealed. Many of the people who had killed others were suffering from nightmares where they constantly heard the screams of their victims, saw their faces as they cried out for mercy and their relatives' agony as they watched helplessly. How could they ever find peace again and live with themselves? Their crimes were replayed in their minds like an endless video. For some, this burden was almost too much to bear.

Deo and John also found that some of the prisoners with whom they talked had an overwhelming desire to meet any surviving victims or the families of those they had murdered, in order to beg forgiveness. The Prison Fellowship felt it was right to organise a conference for prison directors, social workers, personnel who worked with survivors' groups and others who worked with widows' groups. After discussions, the prison authorities allowed such an initiative to be started, which gave teaching and help to both survivors and prisoners. In these discussions a way forward for both groups to find healing was explored. Volunteers were then trained to work within the country's prisons to bring the message of repentance, forgiveness, reconciliation and salvation though the grace of the Lord Jesus.

Prisoners began to respond to the teaching, and soon the government became aware of the results. It was a lifeline – an answer where there had seemed to be no answer. The government then was willing to give more help to the initiative. There is literally a 'captive' audience in a prison! Not only are people physically bound, but also spiritually and emotionally. They have no way to drown out the cries of conscience with drugs, alcohol, sex or other forms of escapism which might be used in the outside world.

The teaching focused on removing the relentless guilt of sin. The only way to regain peace of heart is by the offender taking full responsibility for the sin committed, confessing it first to the Lord, then to the world with real repentance and truly seeking forgiveness. Only when forgiveness has been received can transformation begin in the lives of those who are wounded by their sin.

It wasn't only the prisoners who needed help to find forgiveness. The survivors and the families of the victims needed help, too. Many of them had hearts which were bitter and full of hate and were seeking revenge. The last thing they wanted to do was to forgive those who had committed the atrocities! Why should they? The blood of the victims cried out for justice!

These people needed to understand that ultimately God was the judge, and He would see that justice was done (Romans 12:19). While they held such bitterness and hate in their hearts, they would become spiritually sour and these emotions would become toxic in their lives, eventually bringing sickness and constant pain in their wake, both physically and emotionally.

They would also be in a prison, one of their own making. To be free they had to be willing to forgive and give the right of revenge to God. Only this way would bring them inner healing. Bishop John and Pastor Deo began to train the chaplains and volunteers to work with the three groups. Then began the long process of reconciliation between the groups. It had to happen if there was ever to be a hope that Rwandans could live together in peace once more. This work was not just theoretical teaching; there were many practical issues to address.

Working with the prisoners and preparing them to reintegrate in the outside world, the Prison Fellowship helped those who were illiterate by holding classes to teach reading and writing. These skills would help them to find work after release. There were also sessions aimed to prepare prisoners for the changes which they might find in their nuclear families and in the wider society. Some of the prisoners' wives had deserted them and taken other husbands; others had struggled so much to survive that they had sold the family land. It was the responsibility of the prisoners' families to feed them, and this was a huge burden on some of the wives who were now left without a breadwinner to support them and their children. How could they provide food for their husbands, too?

Sometimes the prisoners had to accept the fact that when they returned home there could be children in the family who had been born to their wives by other men while they were in jail.

Before release the prisoners and volunteers discussed issues like, "How do I tell my children what I did?" They were taught that only true repentance before God and man could break the spiritual curse they had brought upon their children and grandchildren. The country's slogan at every memorial site is 'Never Again'.

This can only be achieved if the curse of genocide is broken. It is a spiritual law, clearly taught in the Old Testament, that God will bring the sins of the fathers onto the children to the third and fourth generation of those that hate Him. True repentance and confession brings not only God's forgiveness, but the breaking of the curse and, instead, the blessing of God for a thousand generations to those that love Him.

Those who feigned repentance and confession of their crimes in order to be released were likely to reoffend in some way. Some prisoners even left prison and murdered again. The prisoners had to be taught to understand these truths.

Along with repentance the prisoners also needed to understand the issues of restitution. Prison Fellowship International has a teaching model called the Sycamore Tree. In 2002 the Rwandan Fellowship adapted this scheme to meet local needs and began to implement it. Six weeks of small group discussions were held with prisoners, led by trained volunteers, followed by two weeks when survivors and family members came and shared their points of view. The discussions were based on the example of Zacchaeus, who, having met Jesus and confessed his sins, then made restitution to those from whom he had stolen.

These discussions were so meaningful that in less than six months from their institution 32,000 prisoners confessed their crimes and accepted Christ into their lives as Saviour and Lord.

In 2002 the practical outworking of this scheme began with the building of the first village of reconciliation, where released prisoners and survivors helped each other to build houses and then to live and work together. The philosophy of repentance had to be worked out in practical, social cohesion. When the houses were built and the people moved in, the new society had to continue to work together to make it an economic success. The village people worked together forming a co-operative, farming or working at some productive project together to make money and rebuild their fractured society. Only a spiritual change in people's hearts could make such a project succeed.*

Bishop John and Pastor Deo took me to see one of the first reconciliation villages. We travelled deep into the countryside in the Musanze district (formerly Ruhengeri) to the village of Kimonyi. In a beautiful valley, under the shadow of the volcanoes, the village of 183 houses was built. We sat near the water pump and soon some of the villagers came to greet us. Their eyes lit up with happiness when they saw John and Deo. First some of the women came to talk, but before long they were joined by men. They came from their plantations and within minutes began to sing and dance. It was obviously a spontaneous eruption of joy and praise as they stopped work to praise God and share with us how well everything was going. Next we were joined by schoolchildren. Some of the villagers had made new marriages and families and there were now children in the community. The children of all the families play happily together.

When the village was built, each household was given a goat and a water tank shared between two households. This was an intentional policy so that, from the beginning, neighbours shared together in the matter of water management.

Although it must have been a long process to rebuild trust, the people in Kimonyi village had managed to do that and were now

---

* See figure 006, page 156

living as a productive community. Recently the government has brought electricity to the village and also given a grant for further development of the economy.

In all, to date, 600,000 homes have been built in reconciliation villages and each one is a thriving, productive community. The work is slow and painstaking, but it has proved that God's forgiveness and love can reunite Tutsi and Hutu again. Jesus is bringing hope to Rwanda!

The government was aware that something had to be changed in order to speed up the justice system. If the prisoners were to be tried in regular courts then it would take well over two hundred years to hear all the cases!

In Rwanda the death penalty was abolished for murder and replaced by a life sentence; however, if all the convicted murderers from the genocide had been given a life sentence, then the circle of hate would just have continued. It was decided soon after the genocide to revive the *gacaca* (pronounced 'gatchatcha') court system that had been used in previous generations in the villages. The idea was that the accused should be tried by the local people in the area where they had committed the crime, and the local people come forward to give witness as to whether or not there was any evidence that such a crime had been committed by that person. If the accused was also willing to confess then the sentence could be reduced by half. When this system was reintroduced it proved a reasonably successful way of trying the genocide prisoners, and although the gacaca court did not itself pass sentence, it led to some people being pardoned when there was no evidence of crime against them. It encouraged the prisoners to admit guilt, and many of those who had repented through the work of the Prison Fellowship did this, having their sentences commuted. These courts continued for some years and speeded up the justice system for many, paving the way for reconciliation.

In 2003 the government declared an amnesty for certain categories of prisoners who had confessed their crimes, and they were released to live again in peace and reconciliation. The work which Bishop John and Pastor Deo had done alongside the prison chaplains and volunteers underpinned this move, so that the prisoners really could be accepted back into the community. Of course there were some who 'confessed' without change of heart, but for many there had been a real change of heart, with repentance towards God and new life in Jesus.

For many years there had been a spiritual darkness hanging over the Great Lakes area of Africa. There have been wars and unrest not only in Rwanda, but in many of the surrounding countries. Only the gospel of Jesus can break through this darkness and bring new life and hope. It has to begin in individuals – one by one, people experiencing a change of heart. Only then can there be transformation and change in a community.

The work of the Prison Fellowship of Rwanda has been recognised by the government to such an extent that they have been asked to screen all other NGOs which have asked to work in prisons. Of course, there has been opposition from inside and outside of the Church. People question the need to continue the work so many years after the genocide. However, there is still an ongoing need for this work. There are still many people in prison whose crimes carry long sentences, and many who have yet to come to repentance and forgiveness.

Even after Bishop John's retirement he was asked if he would still continue his prison work because it was so important, and he agreed to do so. There are still around 55,000 prisoners in jail for genocidal crimes. While there are prisoners, the need for the work remains!

Chapter Twelve

HOPE FOR THE NATION

One of the tragic legacies left by the genocide in Rwanda was the number of orphaned children. In generations past, traditionally any orphaned children would be taken in and nurtured by someone in the extended family, but in the genocide whole family clans were often exterminated, so this just wasn't possible. Children who survived were often left completely alone, with no adult to care for them. Some banded themselves into little family units and cared for each other. I remember the shock, some years ago, when I met a ten-year-old little girl in a tumbledown mud-brick house with a leaky roof. She was valiantly trying to be 'mother' to three younger children. The house was left derelict after the genocide and the children had taken it over and made it their home. They tried to cultivate a few crops in the land around the house, in order to have something to eat. They ran around in old, torn clothes and bare feet. There was no adult to protect them, and no prospect of going to school or ever escaping from their extreme poverty. Always the threat of someone returning to claim the house and land hung over the head of this small 'mother' and she had no idea what she would do if that happened. Mercifully, when a village for such 'child-headed families' was built, a secure home was given to this little family. Scenarios like these could be found all over the country.

Other children were left with only one parent, and without doubt that parent would have been through great trauma. Many of the surviving mothers had been gang-raped in the cruellest way, often resulting in infection by HIV/AIDS. Other families were left with a mother trying to bring up a family while her husband was imprisoned as a result of having committed terrible crimes during the genocide. Many, many families were reduced to living in extreme poverty. Houses were badly damaged, productive land left devastated, electricity and water supplies destroyed, and everywhere there was a feeling of hopelessness as well as mistrust. It was estimated that between 450,000 and 600,000 children were orphaned through the genocide. If nobody addressed the situation and cared for these orphans then Bishop John realised that, as the children grew to adulthood, the situation would be like a time bomb that would eventually lead to further outbreaks of terrible violence. These children had the potential to become a huge, angry army!

What could be done to restore hope to such impoverished communities? This was one of the challenges which faced Bishop John when he began his work in Shyira Diocese. The vision which the Lord gave him for the region was:

1. Evangelism
2. Education
3. Development

The experience which John had gained in Uganda working in mission and evangelism would prove to be an invaluable help as he began to preach the gospel in the diocese and then train, motivate and encourage his pastors to do the same. Only as people heard and responded positively to the gospel could any real change begin. The whole nation was in trauma and grief. It's probably true to say that there was not a family which was untouched by the horror of the genocide. These hearts desperately needed to be touched by the love of Jesus if they were ever to find healing. There was an awareness of spiritual need, but many people found it too hard to trust the leaders of the churches, whatever the denomination might be. At the beginning of the genocide, thousands of people fled to the church buildings to find refuge from the Interahamwe killers, but sadly, were sometimes betrayed by the very people they trusted to help them.

People no longer knew who to trust since many who called themselves Christians had been implicated in one way or another in genocide. Of course, there were some ministers who heroically defended their congregations and were faithful in every way, but equally, there were those who failed under the severe pressure of those days.

It took a lot of time, love and prayer for trust between minister and church members to be restored. There had to be love in action in practical ways for people to then open their hearts to the gospel of Jesus' love. Gradually people began to turn back to the Lord and find the help and healing they needed so badly. There are many packed and vibrant churches in Rwanda today, where people testify to God's healing in their lives.

Adults are often amazed at the resilience of children and their ability to face hardships and continue with their lives. These children most often have some caring adult to help them, but even so, may well need counselling and help in later life. The children from the genocide, however, experienced such extreme trauma and there were so few people able to help them. Bishop John was aware that if there was ever going to be hope for Rwanda, then these children needed to be 'loved' out of their trauma and to be given an education in order that they might have a better life in the future. The future of the nation would, in fact, lie on their shoulders. They needed healing, not just to diffuse the terrible trauma they had experienced, but to remove the curse of violence they had inherited. They also deserved to be given the very best education possible in order to bring about change in their lives and enable them, in due course, to uphold the nation as responsible citizens.

As Bishop John began to pray through the possibility of building a school, a vision emerged of the role that such a school could play within the nation. He saw a school that would be a demonstration school for the whole country. A school where children from all ethnic backgrounds could study together happily and live in reconciliation. A school open to children from the very poorest backgrounds as well as from more affluent homes. A school where pupils learnt to love and respect each other; a school where children moved from a mere existence into motivated, healed and productive lives.

Once the vision had crystallised in Bishop John's mind, he decided he needed to talk to the government official for Community Development and Rehabilitation about implementing it. He hoped that he might be given a grant to cover at least half the cost of such an undertaking. So John made the hazardous journey from Musanze to Kigali. The road winds through the hills, with many hairpin bends, and at that time the tarmac surface was full of potholes, but far more troublesome, it was still subject to rebel-held roadblocks. Having arrived safely, he had the scheduled meeting with the minister. She was a pleasant lady, but poured cold water on all John's plans.

"It's an excellent vision," she admitted, "but far too ambitious for our country at this time. I can give you no help at all and you just can't afford it."

Humbly, John remarked to the Community Development and Rehabilitation officer that if it was just his own idea, then he certainly could not afford it, but if God had given him this vision and if it was to bless Rwanda, then it would happen!

A couple of years later this same lady had to admit to Bishop John that she had been wrong, when she saw that his vision had come to fruition and God had answered his prayers and provided for his needs.

Each year since John had attended the Trinity School of Theology in Pittsburgh, he had been invited back to America to teach and preach. This meant that over the years he had made many friends who knew and trusted him. He could trust them, too, with his vision, and they responded by backing him and helping him in every way they could. Because of this help, Bishop John was able to begin to build a primary school. It was called Sonrise School. The name had been the idea of one of his American friends who, when he heard about the problems of building a school, immediately said, "It must be called Sonrise School, because the Son of God will rise into this situation!"

Chapter Thirteen

HOPE FOR THE CHILDREN
IN SONRISE SCHOOL

Work started on the building of Sonrise Primary School in 1999. Land was obtained just outside the town of Musanze (Ruhengeri), on a hillside. The land was in a perfect and stunning location, once again with the backdrop of the Virunga volcanoes. There are many eucalyptus trees surrounding the campus, giving it a green and pleasant vista. The location is at such a high altitude that mosquitoes are unable to thrive and so the area is malaria-free and also cool at night, which helps everyone to sleep well.

Between 1998 and 2001 over $650,000 was given in donations, by individuals responding as they heard about the need, enabling the school to be constructed.

It took just two years to complete the first stage of the building, a large school with facilities for a maximum of 450 boarding and day pupils. Most of the children are boarders; and the school is a loving home as well as an educational establishment.

Although completed in 2001, the first classes beginning on September 24th with 200 pupils, it was officially opened by the President of Rwanda, His Excellency Paul Kagame, on February 22nd 2002.

In his official speech at the dedication of the school, President Kagame expressed his admiration and gratitude for the tireless work of Bishop John. He commended the bishop "not only as a leader of faith, but as an outstanding citizen and true visionary. Indeed, thousands of Rwandans are reaping the benefit of Bishop John's leadership."

The President presented the school with a gift of a heifer. She was a wonderful cow, giving up to 40 litres of milk a day! This was an amazing provision to help with the children's diets! The cow still serves the school and has provided several offspring who also give very good milk yields.

The official opening was a day of great joy, and those who attended the ceremony, including four members of the USA Sonrise Supporting Team, were greatly blessed.

A fantastic school building is nothing without students! A policy had been devised that would allow only a third of the intake to come from family homes, the other two thirds being orphans. The emphasis, however, was on being a school, not an orphanage, with all the stigma which that name can bring. In the school holidays the children all returned to their village homes.

Bishop John and his team went into the countryside and found children who would not otherwise have been able to attend school. They were the poorest of the poor. He told me about the homes from which they came. The children were often infected with lice, scabies and jiggers. Most had never seen a bed, let alone slept on one! They didn't know what sheets were for. It took a while before some of the children could be persuaded to sleep between sheets on the bunk beds provided in the dormitories. They would curl up on the floor in a blanket, afraid of making the sheets dirty! For the first three months after the school opened, John recalls the matrons repeatedly putting the children back into their beds night after night, until they became accustomed to sleeping that way. Many, too, had no idea how to use a toilet because they had never seen one before they started at Sonrise School. Similarly, they did not know what a toothbrush was for or how to use one. Many had blank stares on their faces, they were so emotionally traumatised. They were very frightened children who needed lots of love and reassurance when they first came to the school. Helping them with basic living skills and giving them reassurance took priority over lessons in the early months. Later their confidence and hope grew and the children began to blossom in their new surroundings. It didn't take too long before the transformation was seen in these children. Soon they had sparkling eyes and beaming faces, were clean, well dressed and well nourished. The loving staff, new friends, nutritious meals, a comfortable bed and regular school schedule with spiritual guidance had worked wonders!

Children from families who were able to afford to do so paid regular school fees and bought the pens, pencil and exercise books which were needed. The orphans were provided for through a sponsorship scheme whereby people in the USA and UK pledged the support needed each month to enable a child to stay at the school. The sponsorship money provided everything required, from the uniform to food or medical fees if a child became sick. This ensured there was no visible difference between the orphans and the other children. They did their lessons together, played together and became friends. This was true, too, whatever ethnic background they originally came from. The children learnt to live together without prejudice and fear. That way there could be hope that when they were grown up they would still respect each other.

There have been many books written about the causes of the genocide and what might have prevented the terrible slaughter of 1994. One clear conclusion at which many writers arrived was that if the general population had been better educated it would have made a significant difference. People would have been able to read the newspapers and be better equipped to think about the issues for themselves and so become less easily deceived by the indoctrination messages which they heard over the radio waves. It became clear that one step which could be taken in order to prevent the ethnic hatred from re-emerging would be to provide educational opportunities for all children in Rwanda. In the years since the genocide the government has worked tirelessly towards this aim, and now every child is entitled to free primary education in a public school and if they are able to pass the primary six examination at a sufficiently high level and progress to senior school, two years' tuition is provided free.

However, that was a long way in the future when Sonrise School was opened, and Sonrise still has a significant role to play as one of the leading schools in the country. Most of the free schools provided by the government are not yet able to reach the standard of teaching which would enable a child to progress through secondary to tertiary education.

Great steps have been made by the government to integrate everyone into one nation. The new flag and new national anthem demonstrate this, as do the new identity cards which have no reference to ethnic grouping but only state that the person belongs to the Republic of Rwanda.

Sonrise School opened for students as soon as the classrooms for primary 1–4 were built. Then, as children completed these school years, the additional classrooms were built for them to continue through years five and six. Once the children had completed year six, and passed the examination, then it was time to leave and progress to senior education. As the first group of students progressed through the school to this level, Bishop John and his colleagues realised that to send them back into the village communities after completing primary school would not fulfil his vision of educated young people becoming the next generation of leaders. So the challenge of building Sonrise Senior School was born! Fortunately there was room on the site to accommodate another school, so plans were drawn up. Fundraising for the senior school* began in 2002, and construction began in late 2003, enabling the first students to enrol in January 2005.

Once again, it was started class by class and it developed as the funds were provided. The first senior class was ready to start as the

---

* See figure 003, page 154

first group of students graduated from primary six. Gradually all the buildings, including a library, computer room and laboratories, were added, making it the impressive school that it is today. The school has a magnificent reputation. The third year of primary six students did so well in the national exams that the school came top in the whole country. It has always been within the top ten schools and often almost at the very top of the leader board! There have now been three groups of students who have graduated from the senior school and the 2014 group are looking forward to their turn to do so in the near future. Many of the senior students who have progressed from Sonrise to university courses are doing very well and still achieving good academic grades.

The vision continues! The diocese has been given land by the government for a Technical University, which will be called Muhabura University, to be built in Musanze. Since Bishop John has now retired, this part of the vision has been handed over to his successor to bring to fruition as funds become available.

In order to maintain the ethos of the school, there has been careful selection and training of all staff, both teaching and ancillary. It is not just an educational establishment, but a place where primarily the children are loved and parented. There is a significant accent on character training and preparation for the pupils to become responsible citizens. Most of all, the children are taught about the love of God for each one of them as an individual and how they can respond to that love, which brings inner healing and transformation. Both the primary and the senior school have a chapel where the children worship together and can learn more of the gospel.

Sonrise School has also gained an international reputation, and now there are pupils whose homes are in Uganda, Congo and Burundi who are enrolled in the school because of both the quality of education and the loving care of the children.

When I visited the schools one thing which impressed me was not just the happy 'buzz' of the young people in their classrooms and

71

walking around the campus, but also the huge organisation needed to keep the school running smoothly. It must be a major employer for the area, which can only be a blessing for the local people. There were cooks and dinner supervisors; women doing the laundry; men chopping firewood for the huge ovens where the cooking was done; stockmen tending the cows; as well as teachers, matrons, nurses, secretaries, security guards and computer technicians! I was told about the men who cut the trees in the forest to bring timber to the campus where it is then sawn up for firewood, and the farm where the vegetables etc. were grown. It made me realise what a vast army was needed to keep the school running so well. Every one of these persons who is involved in the running of the school is, in his or her own way, helping to bring the vision to fruition which Bishop John and Harriet had dared to dream: that of bringing hope to young lives and transforming children into the people God always intended them to be. Bishop John is quoted as saying, "Every child is redeemable, no matter how needy."

Some of the pupils made a book for Bishop John and Harriet in 2011, containing their own tributes. I am quoting from a few that reveal the difference Sonrise has made to their lives, giving them hope for a better future.

"He managed to build a school, 'Sonrise', which has become a home to homeless orphans. He gave shelter and all basic necessities to Rwandan children that had no hope for the future."

"Through that school, the injured children of Rwanda were first [treated] and, having been remade into human beings, school activities began. You can also imagine throughout the first year when the school was opened there was nothing like class work, but only messages of hope were delivered and encouraging words from different people [from] all over the world were shared with Sonrise members."

"I call him [Bishop John Rucyahana] a blessing from God to Rwanda and Africa. Through him God redeemed our nation from the horrors of darkness and the corners of ignorance. One man who managed to heal the wounds and injuries of a multitude of Rwandans."

"He is quoted as being patriotic – yet was never a soldier, never fought for his country with bullets. He fought a war of freeing Rwandans from ignorance – an equally hard war – fighting poverty. A war of re-uniting the country after 1994 genocide, and this man should be put on the list of liberators – heroes of Rwanda."

"Madame Harriet, you wrapped Sonrise kids in your arms and you said 'welcome home'. We shall never forget the way [Harriet] loved us by visiting us daily and gave us advices of all kinds, so that we may be great men and women of tomorrow … you made a vision to give each child a bright hope for a full and productive future."

On the cover of the book of tributes is written:

Someone who
Educated minds,
Broke the cycle of violence
And restored hope.

Chapter Fourteen

HOPE FOR SOCIETY

We read in 1 Corinthians 13:6–7 that "Love … always hopes". Love sees people not just as they are but as they can be through the grace of God. We all need that kind of 'agape' love in our hearts. It is the kind of love which God has for us and the love Jesus demonstrated when He died for us. The more I have thought about hope, and the hope which people in dire situations of poverty, displacement, despair and trauma need, the more I see that hope is grounded in love. Such hope can only be brought into a person's life through another person whose heart is filled with 'agape' love; the self- sacrificial love which cares about people whoever they are, whatever they have done, and sees in them the person they could be by the grace of God, and created in the image of God.

As I write this biography of Bishop John Rucyahana, I know that this love is the basis of his life and work. It is 'agape' love which makes this man and his dear wife the people they are and has helped them to bring so much hope into the lives of those around them, both in Uganda and in Rwanda. Two incidents which occurred while I stayed in their home illustrated this truth to me in a vivid way. They both occurred on the same day.

Bishop John's niece, Rosalie, was sick in Musanze hospital. She had been feeling unwell at the beginning of the week and had gone to the hospital. She was admitted and then diagnosed with acute diabetes. Rosalie's blood sugar was so high that she fell into a coma and John and Harriet stayed with her for many hours in the hospital. Although her blood sugar was later controlled, sadly her kidney function failed and, since the hospital had no dialysis machines, she died. Since Rosalie's father was dead, Bishop John took over all the duties and arranged for the burial and everything else which was needed. They cared lovingly and unstintingly for all the family and friends who gathered round at that time of loss.

Within minutes of hearing of Rosalie's death Bishop John received another phone call. A widow lived in a house opposite the Rucyahana family home. She had been widowed many years before the genocide, but had been forced to leave her home and land in the 1959 exodus and flee to Uganda. She had no children, so when she repatriated to Rwanda after the genocide and found her land and home had been appropriated by others, she had no-one to fight her battle to regain it. By now she was an old lady. She was a member of the Catholic Church, so went to see her priest and asked him to help her get justice. The priest refused to help this old lady and when Bishop John heard the story, he also went to see his colleague, the now former Catholic bishop.

"She is a member of your church and your responsibility," John told the bishop. The bishop still refused to become involved so Bishop John decided to take up her case and help her get back her house and land. He fought her case for fifteen years. The last ten years were fought through the courts and John paid all the legal fees himself. His love persisted and was shown in this practical action, resulting, on that same day as Rosalie died, in a victory for the now ninety-nine-year-old widow. She had been granted justice at long last and the house and land were declared rightfully hers. As Bishop John remarked to me, "At least she can die in peace, knowing God has defended the cause of the widow." Yes, God did, but He did it through His loving servant.

The total destruction in the war left many people in great need and without any visible hope of things improving. Houses and household goods had been wantonly destroyed and people were left without any of the essentials needed for everyday life. When Bishop John moved around his diocese he tried to help those returning from exile to start their lives again. Very ordinary goods were needed, such as plastic cans to carry water; food supplies; soap; second-hand clothing and shoes; spoons, plates, cups, cooking pots and other utensils; blankets and, in some cases, tents for shelter. Providing these very basic items meant that life could be resumed at least to some extent. After a terrible trauma such as these people had experienced, and the constant fear in which they still lived as the Hutu infiltrators' activity continued to threaten their lives from time to time, people needed love and help just to begin to start all over again. When a person experiences such great trauma, it becomes almost impossible to look forward with any hope or enthusiasm; it is all that people can do to just exist from one day to another. John brought hope by supplying these simple essentials. Later, as people recovered further, love and help could be given in different ways.

In the part of his diocese which then was known as Kibuye, in partnership with Christian Aid they were able to give the people 96 cows and 135 goats, to help re-establish animal husbandry. So many animals had been slaughtered in the genocide, which left people with no means of livelihood. The gift of these animals would have made such a huge contribution to the welfare of the people in that district.

Whether communities or individuals, John cares about them all. He has a gift of seeing the potential in a person which can be released to the glory of God. This is shown in a tribute given to me by his personal assistant, Christine Kankindi. In 1997, when Bishop John was settling down into his work in Shyira Diocese, Christine was employed as a cleaner in the diocesan offices. Her education had been cut short due to the genocide, but John could see the potential in this young lady and gave her the opportunity, on two occasions, to attend short courses in computer skills in Kigali. In 2001, Beatrice Mukakalisa, who was Bishop John's personal assistant, was given

77

extended leave from her job because she wanted to pursue full-time further education and gain a degree. That left the Bishop without a secretary.

"You are going to be doing what Beatrice did in my office," Bishop John said to Christine.

"I can't do that," answered Christine. "I didn't finish my secondary education. I'm not qualified!"

"Christine, I have been working with you for many years and you are a person who can learn to do new things," remarked Bishop John. "I saw that capacity in you. I will teach you and help you and show you how things are done."

This is exactly what Bishop John did, gently guiding and helping Christine so that she could cope with the challenges of the new job. She commented that her new boss treated her as a parent would have done.

In 2004, Beatrice returned having completed her bachelor's degree and Bishop John then asked Christine if she would like to return to school and complete her senior schooling. Christine's immediate reaction was, "No, I couldn't do that now."

After a month, Bishop John then asked her again about completing her schooling.

"It's ten years since I had to drop out of school. The education system has changed, and anyway, I have a husband and two children to look after now. I need my salary for us to survive. I really can't think about going to school."

Then Bishop John counselled her again, in his fatherly way. "Christine," he said, "consider this seriously, because the time will come when I will retire from this office and the next person may refuse to employ you because you are not fully educated, even though you have experience. Also, no-one then will remember all the late nights you spent here working for the diocese."

Christine and her husband, who is a pastor, prayed and talked over what the Bishop had said. They agreed that maybe Christine should return to school. So when Bishop John called her for a third time into his office and asked about schooling, she agreed to go. So she was sent to find out all she would need for three years of senior schooling and bring him the list. Having completed her research for this, she gave the list to Bishop John one morning. Then Bishop John had to leave for a meeting in Kigali, but when he returned he asked her to come to his office. He presented her with a cheque to cover all the materials she would need plus the money for three years' school fees.

Christine was totally overwhelmed at his kindness! She did return to school and studied hard for the next three years, sitting the national examination in 1999, and passing with very good grades. Bishop John's faith in her was such an encouragement that, having gained her school leaving diploma, she then wanted to continue her studies at university level.

"It's just one year until my retirement, Christine. Would you be prepared to wait until after I retire before you start studying again? It would be hard for me to get another secretary for just one year."

Christine gladly agreed to wait for another year before she went back to school again.

When Bishop John did retire in 2010, he and Christine talked again about her longing to get a degree.

"Would you be prepared to do your degree by taking evening or weekend classes?" he asked. "Then you could continue as my personal assistant in the ministry work which Harriet and I will be setting up."

So Christine began studying at Bishop Barham University College, Muhabura Centre, in Mbarara, Uganda, at weekends. In March 2014 she completed her studies and graduated with a degree in Development Studies. Since then she has enrolled in a university in Kabale, Uganda, to continue her part-time studies and gain a master's degree. Christine still marvels that she, a cleaner, is now working for a second degree! She is so full of gratitude to Bishop John and his family for all the help which they have given her and the gracious encouragement.

"Our families will remain best friends now and forever!" she said, with joy.

Christine wrote a poem as a tribute to express what she feels about Bishop John:

He is a man of God.
He is a parent.
He is a counsellor.
He loves people.
He loves God.
He is a powerful man, spiritual person.
He loves his nation.
He is a humble person.
He is my best friend.

Christine Kankindi
February 2013

Chapter Fifteen

OFFERING HOPE IN
A HOPELESS SITUATION

Bishop John has a wonderful way of making deep and lasting friendships. It has been already noted in this story that after his period of study in Pittsburgh, he returned every year to America. This was not to raise money for the needy in his parishes, or later for his diocese. Nothing could have been further from John's mind. He was invited back year after year because of the quality of the friendships he made while he was in college and the power with which he preached the gospel when he was invited into the pulpit of the local Episcopal church which he attended.

The love and presence of the Lord which shines out of John's personality made a deep impression on both fellow students and also the minister of the local church where he worshipped. His faith was so vibrant and real, and as such was a great contrast to the 'norm' of Episcopalian Church life in the USA at that time. His faith had been forged in the fires of adversity and glowed red hot, and was based on the fact that the Bible is the revealed, totally trustworthy and inspired Word of God, and within its pages is all we need for salvation and life in Jesus Christ. This was in sharp contrast to the liberalism which was dimming the faith and confusing so many members of the churches of America and Europe, churches which had once been on fire for the Lord and taken the Gospel to the rest of the world, including Africa, in previous generations!

John was invited to preach in churches all over America. At first his ministry started around Pittsburgh, but then spread, as his reputation grew, to a far wider radius. His friends knew about the difficulties faced by many Ugandans after the rule of Idi Amin and later of his successor, Dr. Milton Obote. They knew of the dream of the Mustard Seed Babies' Home in Hoima and urged John to make appeals alongside his preaching, but he would not hear of it. His firm answer was, "I will only preach the gospel. I will not raise funds." The Lord honoured this stand and, without ever giving an appeal, thousands of dollars were given to help the poor of Uganda, and later, Rwanda. It was the Lord's work, and John's confidence that the Lord would provide what was needed was not unfounded. John was not the poor African pastor in need of American dollars! He was not looking for charity or hand-outs, but as a man saved by the grace of God he sought only to share with others the way of true salvation through faith in Jesus. In fact, he became a missionary to the American Episcopal Church at a time when many members had little understanding of the saving gospel of Jesus Christ.

John's yearly visits expanded from six to eight weeks as more and more invitations were given for his evangelistic tours. However, not everyone appreciated his ministry. Sometimes he was criticised and verbally abused. Once, while John was speaking at a conference, a minister was overheard to say to another pastor in the seat next to him (and I quote, with permission, from *Never Silent* by Bishop Thaddeus Barnum, page 36):

> "These Africans are basically ignorant people, aren't they? They believe every word of the Bible. You know what it is, don't you? It is the simple faith of the uneducated. That's all. If only they would come to our seminaries, get a decent education, read the modern theologians, broaden their horizons, and then take it back to their people. What a difference it would be for all of us! This is absurd."

Then the minister smiled, shaking his head and rolling his eyes as if everyone who was anyone would completely agree with his analysis.

"That ignorant African is a friend of mine," the other priest whispered back coldly.

"Sorry?"

"The preacher – John Rucyahana. He's a friend of mine."

"I didn't mean to offend you. But you have to agree –"

"Wait a second," he said, interrupting. "I believe the gospel he is preaching. I believe the Bible is the Word of God, just like him. And here's some trivia for you: Christianity is exploding in his country. People are hearing this same message and coming to faith in Jesus Christ. In many places, they have to hold their services outside because they can't handle the number of people coming to church every Sunday. But here in the United States, Christianity is declining. Our own denomination (Episcopal Church) has lost a third of its membership in the last thirty years. Do you think it's because we're too educated to hear the gospel?"

"Our theological education is better than ever before!" the man retorted.

"Well, let me tell you something about John. He was actually educated in the United States. He went to seminary in Pittsburgh and received a master's degree, just like us. But, thank God, it didn't change him. He is still preaching the gospel message that first changed his life."

He paused for a moment, listening to John preach, then added, "And it changed mine. I think you should listen to him."

The other man fell silent. Afterward, the two men greeted each other cordially and went their respective ways. But what happened between them was not uncommon. The racial prejudice and arrogant tone of the American churchman toward the African Christian surfaced more times than I want to remember.

Indeed, not only was John denigrated and called 'ignorant' and 'primitive', but was accused of visiting the United States only in order to secure money, not just for projects but also to secretly store it away for himself! Others accused John of being power crazy. Anyone who really knew this humble man of God knew how very far from the truth all the accusations were, and in fact John himself, instead of retaliating, prayed for forgiveness for his accusers.

Through his growing friendship with several evangelical Episcopal ministers John became increasingly aware of the dilemmas which they faced within their own dioceses. More and more of the hierarchy of the Episcopal Church were veering away from the Biblical basis and Thirty-Nine Articles of the Anglican Church and adopting the moral ethics of the American society which it was meant to be serving. The Church was no longer the 'salt and light' that it was called to be. The evangelicals were marginalised and very distressed by statements issued by the oversight of their denomination. It was increasingly obvious that they had to make a stand against the heresy which was being widely taught and practised.

In 1997, at the time when John was facing the horrors of post-genocidal Rwanda as a newly consecrated bishop, the situation for the evangelicals in the American Episcopal Church became even more untenable. John cared enough for the brethren there to try to help them.

Bishop Thaddeus Barnum says in *Never Silent* (p. 66): "Why did he care, especially now of all times? He had enough problems back home. Yet, he did care – intensely. As we talked, he listened carefully. Strategically, to the complicated nature of our situation, and offered timely and godly counsel …"

John's friend from schooldays, Emmanuel Kolini, by now had been consecrated as the Archbishop of Rwanda. They discussed the statements issued by the Episcopal Church in America and saw it as a cancer which would, in time, spread throughout the whole Anglican Communion. They advised their American friends they should not keep silent. They had to make a stand against the heresy being taught, even if it cost the ministers their jobs and the churches their buildings, because the Church had to preach the truth of the gospel. Things reached a climax when Bishop John Spong of Newark wrote a statement of belief called the 'Twelve Theses: A Call for a New Reformation'. It was in fact a creed which denied the basic truths of Christianity.

It was against this kind of background, as well as the homosexual issues, that Bishop John encouraged his American friends in the starting of a mission church, St. Andrews, in Little Rock, Arkansas, moving outside the authority of the bishop of Arkansas. Later John was in the forefront of the talks and was a great encouragement to Archbishop Moses Tay of Southeast Asia and Archbishop Emmanuel Kolini of Rwanda when they consecrated two American clergy as bishops to serve under their Provinces as missionary bishops to America.

These and subsequent consecrations took place after much prayer and heart searching, but was the way the Archbishops Tay and Kolini, Bishop John and those in prayer with them were sure God wanted them to respond to the situation in North America. So the AMiA (Anglican Mission in the Americas) was born and has gone from strength to strength, preaching the gospel and bringing many to faith in Jesus.

These godly men from Rwanda, John and Kolini, did not see 'doing nothing' as an option. Their country had gone through genocide and the world had looked on and done nothing. They felt that a spiritual genocide was happening within the Episcopal Church in America and they could not sit on the sidelines and do nothing.

There have been a lot of accusations and misunderstandings over these issues, but it is my belief that John Rucyahana, along with Emmanuel Kolini, Moses Tay and others who were willing to put their reputations and jobs 'on the line', will one day go down in history as the true reformers they are. They are true defenders of the faith. They were willing to come alongside their distressed friends and offer hope where there seemed no hope, and that willingness sprang from their love firstly for the Lord and secondly for the brethren.

Chapter Sixteen

GIVING HOPE TO THE SICK

One of the very sad legacies of war has been the rapid spread of the disease of HIV/AIDS. In the same way that Uganda inherited this legacy after the regime of Idi Amin because rape was part of his army's strategy, so too, tragically, it was a post-genocidal legacy in Rwanda. Rape was part of a deliberate policy, not only to dehumanise and humiliate, but also to infect as many Tutsi women as possible with this terrible disease. It was hoped that any subsequent offspring these poor victims might produce would also be infected with HIV/AIDS and therefore the ethnic group would die out. It was called the 'slow death'. After the genocide 10–11% of the population were known to be infected with HIV/AIDS.

AIDS is a relatively new and dangerous disease which is spread from person to person through the Human Immunodeficiency Virus (HIV). It is found all around the world and is a major cause of death, especially in countries where there is poverty and lack of education or where the general population does not understand the cause and spread of this disease.

The HIV virus can be caught from someone who looks completely well, and it can stay in the body for a very long time before it causes illness. For this reason it is important for people to be tested to see if they have been infected in the past with the virus, so that early treatment can be started. Also, even if they have no symptoms, if they have been infected by the virus they can pass it on to someone else.

The main ways of the spread of the disease are through contact with body fluids, for example through sexual intercourse; using a needle or syringe which someone else has used who has already been infected; or a mother passing the virus through the placenta to her unborn child. These are the usual means of spreading the disease. It is not spread through everyday contact such as shaking hands, playing or eating together. There is much misunderstanding about this, so health education is very important.

Because the virus attacks the immune system, those infected have little ability to fight any other disease with which they might come in contact. The signs and symptoms can be so varied that early detection is sometimes missed. However, if a combination of these three signs is seen, then AIDS should be suspected and the tests carried out:

1. Gradual weight loss, so that the person becomes thinner and thinner
2. Diarrhea for more than 1 month
3. A fever which may come and go for more than 1 month

Although there is no cure for AIDS, much can be done to help and care for the sufferers. This is where concerned individuals like Bishop John have been able to help so much. In Shyira Diocese, in partnership with PFI he helped to organise training in Musanze and Gakenke so that people could understand and fight this killer disease. HIV/AIDS has been a disease which not all churchmen have wanted to discuss or address because of the connection with promiscuous sexual activity. Embarrassment, leading to 'sweeping the issue under the carpet', only helps the disease to proliferate. Bishop John understood that it needed to be discussed 'in the open', and sufferers need the love and support of the Christian people around them as they face a long, slow death. So much misunderstanding about the nature and spread of the disease has resulted in patients being ostracised and isolated, instead of being loved and helped. Whether or not a person is an innocent victim of the disease, they need to know the love of Christ and to have the practical help of people in the community as well as medical treatment to help keep them as well as possible for as long as possible. It needs leaders like Bishop John to be involved in the fight against HIV/AIDS, as he was willing to be.

As well as the training programme, Bishop John set up a youth voluntary testing centre in Musanze. Here, a young person is able, in complete confidentiality, to go for a test to see if they have been infected by the virus. Such a centre is so important for these young people. If the virus is detected then the Government of Rwanda provides free treatment with anti-retroviral drugs, which can prolong life for many years. However, if these drugs are prescribed then the person may require help to buy food as they need to eat a great deal while they are being treated. This, again, is an area where the Christians can show love to the hurting in their community by helping to provide the needed extra food.

This was not the only health issue in which Bishop John became involved. The mission station of Shyira had been founded many years before by British CMS missionaries who were allowed to extend their work from Uganda into Rwanda. Among the group were some medical personnel who had a great concern for the health of the local people. They were given the site of Shyira Hill, located forty miles east of Gisenyi and fifteen miles south of Musanze, as a place on which to build a mission station. This was established in 1929 and it became one of the places where the Lord moved through His Spirit in a remarkable way and the East African Revival began. A church, school and hospital were built there. The hospital served the local community very well for many years, but began to decline in the late 1980s.

It was geographically in a very vulnerable position, being quite near the border with Congo. This meant that it suffered severe damage during the genocide and afterwards, until the fighting in that area stopped around 1998. After Bishop John settled into the diocese he began to organise the rebuilding of the hospital, which had been left as nothing more than a ruin and had no doctors serving it.

Since 2003 it has been completely transformed into a good, functional district hospital which serves not just the Shyira community, but also the surrounding hill country beyond. It has, as well as general hospital facilities, a maternity block, paediatric unit, laboratory, operating theatre, some private wards, a hospice and a specialised treatment centre for malnutrition. There are thirteen satellite health centres served by the main hospital, and although the surrounding roads are very rough and local transport is still erratic, it provides a quality of medical care hard to find in most rural parts of Rwanda.

As well as the rebuilding of Shyira Hospital, the Rwandan Government donated to the diocese some old houses in a place called Bigogwe. In the past these had been used by the army, but were no longer required. Bishop John had the vision to build a community facility there. He built a primary and a secondary school, a hall for conferences and meetings, and also a health centre. He was able to build this health centre with the help of partners, especially an English couple, Dr. and Mrs. James Derrick. Another health centre was then constructed at Nyange, and two dispensaries in the villages of Kimonyi and Nyiragikokora. It was no mean feat to undertake such big projects at a time when the country had little money and a multitude of problems to address. Caring for the health of the people in his diocese was very important to Bishop John. His work was, and still is, a holistic ministry in the widest sense. Preaching the gospel was always the priority, but loving and bringing hope to hurting people of every kind was equally part of that message.

Chapter Seventeen

STRENGTHENING HOPE
IN THE NATION

Rwanda may have been left with a wonderful spiritual legacy of revival which later spread into all of East Africa, but sadly, she, along with so many other countries in the world, has also been left with a toxic legacy from the empire building of the colonialist era. Of course it would be naïve to assume that all of Rwanda's political troubles stemmed from the colonial rule of first Germany, then Belgium. However, the policies introduced through these decades did lay a foundation of hatred between the ethnic groups within the country.

Bishop John feels very strongly that fifty years on from independence, the nation, indeed Africa as a whole, needs to stop blaming all of the present political upheaval on the colonial past; the countries must become accountable for their present. Looking back since independence, many years have been worse than the years when they were controlled by a colonial power. John knows that it is time for Rwanda to take responsibility for the future of the nation, and not always put blame on others, in order to regain the dignity and shape the destiny of the nation.

"To obtain dignity is a struggle. It is not an instant commodity which can be taken off a supermarket shelf," Bishop John explains to me as we talk about the issues. "Everyone has to work for dignity.

Where there is violence and corruption it will not occur. As a country we need to be both accountable and responsible, so that our poor children do not remain poor. Relief and hand-outs cannot make our economy flourish. We have to get to work with whatever resources we already have and then share the results with others. Only this way can we make our country grow!"

In a way this echoes something written in the World Health Organization's *World Report on Violence and Health* (E.G. Krug et al., eds. Geneva: WHO, 2002): "Safety and security don't just happen; they are the result of collective consensus and public involvement."

It takes a change of thinking not just by the leaders of a nation or group, but also by the people at the grass roots, for new attitudes and policies to happen. History shows us that children brought up with violence resign themselves to it and accept it as normal, so they in turn are likely to use violence as a weapon. People need hope to believe that a better future is possible before they will take responsibility for helping to change it or their destiny.

The three people groups of Rwanda – Tutsi, Hutu and Twa – co-existed and lived together in reasonable harmony for many centuries before the colonial era. They were ruled by their kings, called *Mwami* in Kinyarwanda, the one language spoken by all the people of the nation. Society was headed up by local chieftains of thirteen clans, who although they led and held authority among their own people, were all subject to the king. The Twa people are related to the pygmy people of the Congo, but the origin of the Hutu and Tutsi is lost in the mists of time and although legends persist, the truth is not known. The history of the nation was handed down orally from father to son, and truth has become obscured through the ages. For the past four years Bishop John has been undertaking research which proves that some Hutus and Tutsis share the same family tree, which may have resulted in the social classes which later developed. As all the people spoke the same language, and shared the same culture and religion, the only clear distinction was vocational because the Tutsi were cattle keepers and the Hutu tilled the land, while the Twa were hunter-gatherers and skilled in making pots. In fact, the definition of a Tutsi was a person who owned more than ten head of cattle. Possibly because of the milk which the Tutsi children were able to drink, the members of this group on the whole were taller than the Hutu. The kings were normally from the Tutsi, but they intermarried and so many of their wives were Hutu. It is historically clear that there were no strong divisions between the people. Disputes were settled by the king with the help of leaders and this enabled his people to live together in harmony.

The king's traditional palace was a round grass-roofed hut. Outside was a low mud-brick wall, where his people could sit and bring their complaints to the king, who sat at the entrance on a low stool to listen and make judgments.

When Europeans began to make explorations into Africa, in the late 1880s, some German missionaries entered Rwanda. Because of the location of this small country, right in the centre of the African continent and surrounded by mountains and hills, it had remained untouched by the slave traders who had traversed Africa before that time. Germany then claimed Rwanda as one of its territories, and the power of the Mwami began to wane. The Germans had always had an interest in tribal origins, such as their own Aryan ethnic origins, and they began to divide the people into the three ethnic groups which we know today.

After the First World War the German territories were divided up and given to other nations. Since the Belgians held the neighbouring territory of Congo, the League of Nations gave Rwanda to them. Belgium already had a mixed culture with racial distinctions between the French-speaking and Dutch-speaking people in their homeland, and they continued such distinctions between the Tutsi, Hutu and Twa when they ruled Rwanda.

The colonial rule affected every part of a citizen's life, cultural, educational and religious. Those defined as Tutsi, by the number of cows they owned, became the 'ruling' class and privileged. They had greater access to education. The schools were all under the auspices of the Catholic Church, and here the class divisions were upheld and so ethnic hatred was fostered. This divide between the people grew as the forty years of colonial rule continued. The Hutu were far more numerous than the Tutsi or Twa, so when free elections took place in 1962 at the end of Belgian rule, the Hutu, government-backed party was certain to get a majority and gain power. With a Hutu majority in the government and the nursing of three decades of hatred against the Tutsi, the seedbed was laid for the harvest of genocide. As the hatred intensified, violence erupted in 1959, then sporadically through the next thirty-five years, culminating in the genocide of 1994.

To counteract the hatred and mistrust between peoples after the genocide would be no easy task for the incoming government. Divisive attitudes were by now deeply imbedded into the national culture, and those who had survived genocide were extremely traumatised. The land was bloodstained and fear of recurrence or reprisals made attempts at reuniting the country almost impossible. Even within the Church there was often fear and hatred. This is why Bishop John faced such a difficult task when he was consecrated as Bishop of Shyira Diocese. It was not just devastated infrastructure and poverty which he needed to address, but fear, anger and hate. The needs were overwhelming. It was not just the Anglican Diocese of Shyira which needed healing, but every parish and every church community of every denomination.

To illustrate the fear and trauma that Christians, along with everyone else, were experiencing, I will retell part of the experience of a Pastor, Rev. Stephen Gahigi, as told in an earlier book of mine, *After Genocide – There Is Hope* (Mary Weeks Millard, Terra Nova Publications, 2006).

Pastor Stephen lived and worked in a parish called Mbyo in the region of Bugesera. It was an area where there was a high proportion of Tutsi people living, so it was a prime target for the perpetrators of genocide. Out of his family clan, numbering just over one hundred, eighty-six people died. Stephen was trying to get his nuclear family and some other close relatives to safety in Burundi. It was April 7th 1994, the day of the plane crash which killed the presidents of Burundi and Rwanda and unleashed the planned genocide. They travelled that night through the bush but were ambushed by government soldiers and local militia who were on a killing spree. Stephen's wife, Francine, had their youngest baby girl strapped to her back, Stephen's sister carried their one-year-old daughter in a similar way, and Stephen himself had Claude, their five-year-old son. Together with thirty or so other relatives they made their way in the dark and torrential rain to the Burundi border. They were about half an hour's walk away when the soldiers waiting in ambush opened fire on the group. It was mayhem, with screams from the injured and dying, and anyone who was able fleeing into the nearby bush. Six who managed to run away were quickly caught by the Interahamwe (local militia) and frogmarched all the way back to their village, only to be hacked to death by machetes when they arrived. Just five of the group managed to escape, Stephen being one of that number.

Stephen prayed as he hid in the bush. Daylight was approaching quickly and he felt he should try to continue the journey to safety. All seemed quiet around him. In order to get back on to the path which led to the border, Stephen had to retrace his steps to the scene of the massacre. He couldn't even bear to look at where his family lay, but he thought he heard a baby's cry. In horror and shock he searched among the dead and found it was his own daughter who was crying, still strapped to her aunt's back. Stephen's sister was dead. He untied his little girl and then decided he had to search and see if anyone else was alive before he ventured on. It seemed everyone was dead. Stephen began to leave the scene of horror. Then he felt as if eyes were looking at him, and felt a compulsion to go back. He found his son, Claude, covered in blood. He had been shot in the arm.

Blinded by tears, he had to leave the place in haste, not even being able to bury his loved ones as the soldiers could still be around and by now it was almost light. He put his daughter on his back, just as a woman would do, as he needed to carry Claude in his arms. His son was crying for a drink and in desperation Stephen scooped up some water from a puddle in order to quench his thirst. By a miracle his son didn't get sick from that water.

About 300 metres from the border he was about to make a run for it when he heard a noise and saw Interahamwe militia near him. Had he come this far, just to die? He hid again, the children miraculously quiet. The Interahamwe had seen Stephen, but thought he must have gone down a small, nearby path to escape them, so they chased after him that way. As soon as they were out of sight he ran as best he could and reached the safety of the border.

Later, in a refugee camp, he was delighted to find that his wife and baby daughter were also alive, the only other survivors of the group.

After his escape Stephen held a lot of hurt and bitterness in his heart and a lot of questions for God. In the refugee camp and also when he worshipped at a local Burundian church, Stephen knew that the Lord was speaking to him and calling him to return to Rwanda in the wake of the genocide and preach to the Hutu who had been imprisoned for their involvement in the genocide. It was a great battle for him to obey the Lord, but Stephen and Francine did return. They found all their family property razed to the ground, all their cattle killed, almost every relative dead. The few widows and orphans who survived were now his responsibility.

Having returned, it took Stephen a long time before he felt able to go to the prison and preach there. When he did, the prisoners didn't want him near them. They recognised him as the local pastor and thought he was spying on them. He persevered because he was sure the Lord was telling him to preach in the prison. He prayed and prayed to find the strength to forgive the killers. In the course of time there was a response to his preaching, and prisoners began to repent, confess their sins and ask the Lord for forgiveness. One of these was a man who confessed to the murder of his sister that night on the path to Burundi. Stephen, by God's grace, was able to forgive this man, and eventually, when he was released, the two men worked together in reconciliation and preaching the gospel. There is far more to this story, but it shows the depth of trauma which was common to so many in the country, and that even as a Christian, it was not an easy road for Stephen to obey the Lord and visit the prison and even more difficult to actually forgive the one who had murdered his sister.

Bishop John has his own similar struggle to face, for although he was not in Rwanda during the genocide, an incident occurred just after his return. He had a niece, living in the area, who had recently come to visit him and Harriet. The area around Musanze was still very unstable due to attacks by Hutu infiltrators from the Congo. Very soon after the visit, Bishop John's niece was brutally murdered. He was left traumatised, angry and full of hate for the attackers. Bishop John and Harriet had to come to the place where, at the foot of the cross of Jesus, they could lay down the burden of bitterness and hate and choose to forgive the attackers. This is a difficult spiritual journey to make; but having done it, John was then able to reach out to men in the prisons and truly show them love and preach forgiveness in Jesus' name.

Impossible as it may seem after the horror of genocide, by the mercy of God and through the faithful preaching of the gospel along with love shown in social, practical action, the healing of individual hearts and of a nation slowly began. The dream of unity and reconciliation had started and so hope was born that one day it would become a reality.

Chapter Eighteen

HOPE FOR HEALING
OF TRAUMA

When we reflect on wars such as the Rwandan genocide, we can see how the prince of this world, Satan, tries to destroy nations. Equally, as we reflect on the toxic legacy which such conflicts leave, we can see how he tries also to destroy the lives of individual survivors through the trauma they experience. Then we can reflect on God's purposes which are always to bring healing, restoration and transformation both to nations and to individuals.

In retelling the story of Stephen Gahigi, I am reminded of the traumatic legacy which his son Claude carries even to this day. Although he was only five years old at the time of the ambush, his life was so impacted by the trauma that, as he grew up and went to school, his ability to learn was severely diminished, although there has been no apparent educational or medical reason for this. He struggled for many years to complete his primary schooling and has been unable to progress beyond that stage.

Another friend of mine was widowed in the genocide. Her husband and youngest son were murdered while she and her other two sons were away from their home. Many other relatives including her parents were also killed. Left with her two sons to provide for, this dear lady went to Kigali and eventually found work within the

Anglican Church. Her eldest son managed to resume his schooling and in time completed secondary education and entered university. The younger surviving son was a five-year-old when his father and brother were murdered. His life since that time has been dogged with periods of severe trauma and depression resulting in long absences from school. Counselling and psychiatric drugs have done little to really help this young man, although, through the love, patience and prayers of his mother and her church family, he has now, after eighteen years, been able to complete his secondary schooling and is looking forward to eventually entering a university where he can study music, although at the present time such facilities are unavailable in Rwanda. Although he is coping with his disabilities to some extent, he and his family know that he is not yet completely healed, and continue to pray for him that by God's grace and in due course he will be totally well.

These are not two isolated cases; there are many people, both young and old, who still have a deep-seated trauma that stems from what they saw or experienced during the genocide. The psychiatric services of the country are woefully inadequate to cope with the ongoing legacy of toxic emotions left by the war. Twenty years is a comparatively short time when it comes to human memory and traumatic damage. Even in these days of greater understanding of 'post-traumatic stress syndrome', and counselling services geared to help sufferers, it may take years to bring healing to the tortured mind.

I was reminded of this very dramatically through an incident in my own life about ten years ago. I was born during World War Two, and have only a few clear memories of my early childhood and of the actual war, although I can remember the post-war years, living among bombed-out buildings and enduring food shortages etc.

In 2013 I was visiting Uganda and helping with an evangelistic mission in a village community. Meetings were held during the day, with choirs singing, testimonies given and the Word of God preached. It was a joy to see many people repent and come to faith in

Jesus. At the end of the day, we travelled to a nearby town and slept in a sort of guest house. Our bedrooms were individual mud-brick rooms with corrugated tin roofs. Inside each room was a bed and a chair. There was one very small window, which had wooden shutters, and they, when closed, obscured all light. The door was metal and was bolted and locked from the inside. I felt a little claustrophobic in the room, and even more so after I had tucked the mosquito net around the mattress, although I was not too sure why I had bothered to do this, it had so many holes in it!

I spent a while in prayer and thanksgiving for all the blessings of the day, then switched off my torch and tried to sleep. For several hours sleep evaded me, so rather than 'count sheep' I began to talk to the Shepherd, and finally I dropped off into the kind of really deep slumber that happens at the end of a wakeful period.

About 5am I was suddenly awakened by a very loud noise and what to me sounded like gunfire! A few flashes of brilliant light managed to filter through the tiny cracks around the window shutters, the holes in the tin roof and under the door. I was terrified and totally disorientated. The panic and trauma I experienced was enormous and all normal, logical thought was gone. I wasn't aware of the Lord or even able to articulate a cry to Him. I had no idea what was happening to me, only an utter terror that was somehow familiar yet utterly alien at the same time.

That terror could have only lasted for a few minutes and then reason took over, but it seemed like hours.

As the trauma and panic subsided, I realised that I had been awakened by a tremendous thunderstorm, with hail that sounded like bullets falling on the tin roof, and lightning that flashed through the tiniest space under the door and window shutter and even odd small holes in the roof.

As I calmed down I began to ask the Lord what had happened to me. Why had I reacted in the way I had? I had learnt through the years to ask the Lord to show me the reason if I was aware that in any situation I had overreacted. Usually there was a spiritual root cause.

Suddenly I knew that this deep, hidden trauma within me was a 'left over' reaction from the war. It was a 'throwback' to the time when as a baby I was rushed into air-raid shelters when the German bombers attacked.

A week or so later, when I was back in England, I knew I needed to explore this trauma with the Lord. The war had been sixty years previous and yet I was still suffering from the effects. My own experience as a counsellor told me that it would always remain in my psyche as a time bomb ready to explode given the right circumstances, unless I could defuse it with the Lord. Hidden trauma, if unrecognised, is able to cause many illnesses like high blood pressure and heart disease, diabetes and cancer.

I spent time in prayer, reliving the feelings of terror I had experienced in Uganda, and accepting the fact that I had harboured this pain since early childhood. I then mentally gave the problem to the Lord, laying it at the foot of His cross, and asking him to bring the inner healing I needed from that time of trauma. I asked the Lord to make it as if it had never happened in my life. I would always retain the memory, but not the trauma and pain.

I was very grateful because I knew from past experience how to deal with trauma like this. Between the ages of seven and eleven I had been regularly sexually abused. I suppose my experience, compared with the abuse and rape which women endured in the genocide, might not seem so terrible, but any violation of this kind always damages a person and causes deep trauma. Like many other young girls who experience such an ordeal, as I grew up I hid it deep within my psyche and built defence mechanisms around me to help me cope with life. There came a time many years later when the hidden trauma surfaced and began to cause emotional pain, damaging my ability to live my life normally. It was then that I was helped by a Christian counsellor to allow the trauma and pain to rise to the surface, to acknowledge it and to give it to the Lord. Then came the battle to choose to forgive the perpetrator and give him to God. I gave up any right I might have for revenge, believing the scripture in Romans 12:19, where the Lord says, "Vengeance is mine, I will repay" (KJV).

I found healing and was left with just a memory from which the toxic trauma had been removed.

Now I can look back on these events, even grateful for them, for not only have they made me the person that I am today, but they have helped me to understand, to some small extent, the trauma which my brothers and sisters in Rwanda have endured and to know that in Jesus there is healing and hope.

Unless the survivors of genocide find this healing, then the trauma will remain with them through their lives, a time bomb ready to explode into serious illness of one kind or another in future years.

Every time a person's senses remind them of a past traumatic event, they can be sent into terror and panic such as I experienced that morning in Uganda.

Each April a week of mourning is held in Rwanda to remember the beginning of the terrible events which began on April 7th 1994. I am sure it is appropriate for people to take this time to remember, in the same way as we in Britain hold our Festival of Remembrance on November 11th each year and thank God for deliverance from war.

I had the privilege of attending the Mourning Day one year at a venue between Cyangugu and Kibuye. It was very moving. However, as one wreath was laid by a Catholic nun, a lady near me dissolved into terror and trauma. What she felt echoed in my heart. She was gently taken away into a first-aid tent, where others were being treated for similar eruptions of traumatic memories. I asked what had caused her to be so overcome, and it was explained to me that the nun placing the wreath had been someone who had betrayed this woman's family to the Interahamwe, thus causing their deaths. The visual recognition had sent her into trauma, much as the sound of the thunderstorm had triggered the trauma within me. Sometimes a smell, touch or a taste can also bring such a vivid toxic memory to a person and throw them into trauma.

I asked what treatment would be given to the poor woman who had been taken to the tent, and was told, "She'll have an injection which will put her to sleep. When she wakes up, she will have forgotten again."

This made me so sad. I knew the medical services had little to offer because the scale of the legacy of trauma was so huge. However, I also knew that pushing the memories down once again was no cure. It only gave the woman a little temporary peace.

How I thank God for the ministry of Bishop John and others like him who share the truth that there is hope for inner healing when we bring our burdens and are willing to expose our hurts to Jesus. Afterwards there always follows the walk along the hard road to offer forgiveness to those who have sinned against us.

Having shared some of my personal experience in this chapter, it seems appropriate to end with the Prayer of Preparation at the start of the Holy Communion service taken from the *Common Worship* Service Book of the Church of England, for only the Holy Spirit knows the deep secrets of our hearts and can deal with them.

> Almighty God,
> To whom all hearts are open,
> All desires known,
> And from whom no secrets are hidden:
> Cleanse the thoughts of our hearts
> By the inspiration of your Holy Spirit,
> That we may perfectly love you,
> And worthily magnify your holy name;
> Through Christ our Lord. Amen.

Chapter Nineteen

HOPE THROUGH NATIONAL UNITY AND RECONCILIATION

Bishop John Rucyahana will be remembered both in Uganda and Rwanda as a Christian leader who has made a great contribution to the Anglican Church in these countries. In Rwanda, he will also be remembered for his contribution as a devoted citizen and leader of his people, especially in the area of reconciliation and unity.

In April 2010, on his retirement as bishop, he was invited by the Rwandan government to be President of the National Unity and Reconciliation Commission (NURC). He accepted the post and has served in this position in an honorary capacity ever since.

Before the genocide, when racial tensions in Rwanda were beginning to come to a head, meetings were held in Arusha, Tanzania, called by the OAU (Organisation of African Unity), to try to diffuse the situation. As a result of these talks the Arusha Peace Accord was signed in 1993, and one of the recommendations in it was that a Commission for National Unity and Reconciliation be established to help the Rwandese Government find a way through the crisis. This commission was to foster a spirit of unity among the people of Rwanda, who through the years of bad governance had known racial divisions, discrimination, human rights abuse and acts of violence.

In August 1993, President Habyarimana of Rwanda was pressurised into attending the talks in Arusha by an ever increasing international demand for democratisation of his government and also by the military successes of the RPF (Rwandese Patriotic Front) which could no longer be ignored. The ten days of talks in Arusha produced a series of protocols which aimed at reducing the powers of the presidency and promoting greater power sharing, and the integration of the RPF into the armed forces to such an extent that 40% of the lower ranks and 50% of the officer ranks would be comprised of their troops. It was under huge international pressure that President Habyarimana reluctantly signed the agreement. For him, it was almost like signing his death warrant. The proposed commission for unity and reconciliation was never set up.

The President was returning to Rwanda after a further round of talks in Arusha on April 6th 1994 when his plane was shot down, killing both him and also the President of Burundi who was travelling with him. The next day the genocide began.

After the genocide, once peace and orderly government was re-established, it was even more necessary that the original recommendation of the Arusha Peace Accord was implemented. So the Rwandan government passed a law, No. 03/99 on March 12th 1999, to establish a National Unity and Reconciliation Commission. It was given the responsibility to use all possible means to bring about real unity and reconciliation among the people of Rwanda. What a task lay ahead for the members of this commission! There were so many divisions because of the life experiences of the populace. Firstly, there were the survivors of genocide. The members of this group were deeply traumatised and their families decimated by the genocide. Then there were also thousands of Rwandans imprisoned for their part in the genocide, and their families who were left in their homes and villages, terrified that they might face reprisals. A third group was made up of exiles returning from the surrounding countries to which they had fled for refuge during 1994. Still others were repatriating after many years of being refugees all around the world. Some of these were from a new generation of Rwandans who had been born and grown up outside their homeland, and who knew English rather than French as their second and educational language. How could unity and reconciliation be brought to such a divided nation as this?

The constitutional responsibilities of the NURC are as follows:

1. Preparing and co-coordinating the national programme for the promotion of National Unity and Reconciliation
2. Putting in place and developing ways and means to restore and consolidate Unity and Reconciliation among Rwandans
3. Educating and mobilising the population on matters relating to National Unity and Reconciliation
4. Carrying out research, organising debates, disseminating ideas and making publications relating to peace, National Unity and Reconciliation
5. Making proposals on measures that can eradicate divisions among Rwandans and to reinforce National Unity and Reconciliation
6. Denouncing and fighting against acts, writings and utterances which are intended to promote any kind of discrimination, intolerance or xenophobia
7. Making an annual report and such other reports as may be necessary on the situation of National Unity and Reconciliation
8. Monitoring how public institutions, leaders and the population in general comply with the National Unity and Reconciliation policy and principles.

Unlike other commissions of its type, the NURC did not have a truth-finding brief to fulfil as the ICTR (International Criminal Tribunal for Rwanda) and Gacaca court process was undertaking this task. The commission could therefore concentrate on finding ways to reach its goal of reconciliation between the differing groups of people. It decided to progress in four ways.

1. Peace Building and Reconciliation Programme

The commission aimed this initiative at the general population of the country. They wanted to create forums where the issues of race and reconciliation could be openly discussed and give people the opportunity to air their feelings and their views. This would enable the deeply held perceptions and views of the past to be discussed in a non-threatening environment as well as examining how the people felt in the present, and what their hopes and dreams might be for the future of their country. Just as the sectarian views had gradually encroached on the collective mind of the Rwandan nation over many years, so it would take time to combat these views and promote respect for all people and their human rights. The commission used various approaches to promote such open debate: seminars, conferences, debates broadcast both on radio and television, and meetings in all the regions of the country. The NURC also conducted a survey of the popular opinion in all 106 districts of Rwanda, hoping to get a true picture of how people felt and what they thought. It was important that the general populace knew that their opinions counted and that their government was listening to them.

Another part of this initiative has been the *Ingando* (solidarity) camps. These camps are run for forty-five days and are meant to bring together different groups of people. Newly returned emigrants are encouraged to attend to ensure their safety and also help them to understand the recent history of Rwanda and the new climate of reconciliation which is being fostered. The principles of peaceful co-existence, tolerance and good governance are explored.

Young people, teachers, youth workers, government workers, doctors, and those suspected of having been involved in genocide and who are paroled are also groups who attend the camps. They are mandatory, too, for all new university students who receive state-funded scholarships.

The Ingando are jointly administered and run by NURC and Rwandan political figures.

Part of the programme consists of visits to some of the genocide memorial sites, so that the participants can see for themselves something of the scale and horror of the slaughter. I am sure that the 'Never Again' slogan will forever ring in their ears, having visited those sites. The impact of visiting such sites makes a deep and lasting impression on people's hearts. There have been those who would deny that genocide ever took place, but no-one who has visited the memorials could ever doubt the veracity of what happened.

2. Support for community-based initiatives

The commission gives support and encouragement to all community-based schemes to help alleviate poverty and rebuild wholesome communities. People living in unrelieved poverty without any hope of their lifestyle improving are less likely to live in harmony and reconciliation. The NURC gives financial support to more than sixty non-profit-making community development initiatives to help improve the lives of the poor. The members of these groups include both survivors and perpetrators of genocide, and people whose family members are in prison.

In schools and universities Reconciliation Clubs have been started, where students of every ethnic group can meet and befriend each other and learn to live, work and play together as fellow Rwandans. As well as these government-initiated clubs, some student bodies have also formed their own associations, e.g. the Student Club for Unity and Reconciliation (SCUR). These clubs also organise visits to the genocide memorial sites to honour the victims and reinforce the 'Never Again' message.

The support given by the NURC includes instructors and advisors travelling throughout the country to help such clubs become established and the provision of educational materials for the groups' activities.

3. The National Summit

The first summit was held in 2000. It was very successful so further summits have continued bi-annually. Led by the commission's president, they have been seen as the star project of the NURC. It is Bishop John's role, among others, to prepare for these, for as president he leads each summit while he remains in office. The purpose of the summit is to bring together the people of Rwanda, as well as important people from the international community. It is a public forum which informs the world of the continuing progress and achievements of the NURC. It also allows debate and invites suggestions and recommendations as to how the commission's goals can be better developed and achieved in the future. The sole aim is to continue to encourage and bring unity and reconciliation to all strata of life in Rwanda.

4. Community festivals

Community festivals are held each year, birthed and supported by the Commission. These have an important part to play in reconciliation through theatre, music, dance and art. These festivals strengthen unity and social transformation among the people of Rwanda. Rwandans have a vibrant culture with great traditions of drumming, dancing and singing. As in the churches, many traditional dances and songs have been given new words and movements which help the congregations to express their love for God, so for these festivals, songs and dances have been written and choreographed to help strengthen the positive message of reconciliation.

When in 2006 I attended the twelfth Mourning Day anniversary of the genocide, I was given a leaflet produced by the Ministry of Youth, Culture and Sports. At that time the Gacaca courts were still in operation. Since then, their work has been completed. On the front of the leaflet it stated:

> Let's commemorate the genocide in actively taking part
> in Gacaca courts and having the bravery to tell the truth

and to be resilient, overcoming the consequences of the genocide.

The memorial service was being held in the district of Nyamasheke in western Rwanda. The final paragraph of the leaflet stated:

> Nowadays, the population seems to have understood that Rwandans have to live together again. This appears especially in the fact that the associations that are created do not have any form of discrimination.

> Concerning Gacaca, people have reached a satisfactory stage. The number of those who confess and plead guilty is 70%. Nyamasheke is one of the Districts with a high rate of those who have confessed and accepted their crimes. Today, women whose imprisoned husbands are reluctant to confess, advise their husbands to confess and plead guilty.

These are quite amazing statements which demonstrate that even as early as 2006 much progress had been made through the work of the NURC. The work still continues and will need to do so for many years to come. The rising generation needs to be taught and understand how it was that the years of racial hatred and then genocide occurred, as well as being taught the positive ways to live together in unity and reconciliation. Thank God these issues are being addressed by the Church, but also that the Church is part of the political process, too.

Such a work must delight the heart of God, who longs that all people live together in unity, respect and peace. It is wonderful that a man of God has been chosen and is willing to serve his country in this way. It is by no means an easy task, especially in retirement, but the Lord has called his people to be peacemakers. May Bishop John indeed be blessed in this role as he serves both his Lord and Rwanda.

"Blessed are the peacemakers, for they will be called sons of God."
Matthew 5:9

Chapter Twenty

BUILDING IN HOPE

When John was still a boy at school he had dreams of being an engineer, then later on this changed to wanting to be a geologist. Although those dreams were not fulfilled because his education was cut short due to the political situation, his love of buildings and construction found fulfilment in various projects which he undertook in later life. Earlier in this story I mentioned the construction of the reconciliation village in Kimonyi, built in partnership with the Prison Fellowship. The same partnership also built a smaller village of twenty houses at Karwasa for survivors of the genocide.

There is always so much rebuilding and reconstruction work needed after a war. I have many memories of walking along roads in the city where I lived as a child. Alongside very nice houses there would be a space or a ruin, where a bomb had fallen, causing destruction. These bomb sites became our playgrounds even though they were very unsafe. Even in the play space at my senior school there was a huge bomb crater. So many reminders of the war were depressing and demoralising for the people who lived around them. It took a long time for England as a nation to recover and eventually be able to rebuild homes and indeed whole cities. It has been the same for Rwanda. Someone was needed with vision to address the need and help build homes for the dispossessed. Bishop John, with help from the Norwegian Church Aid, organised the building of 150 houses in Shyira Parish, 150 houses at both Gitare and Nyiragikokora, and a further 220 homes in the town of Musanze. In order to achieve this construction work, a training programme had to be introduced for people to learn the necessary basic building skills. Over a thousand people who were trained in masonry and construction are now supporting themselves and their families as they continue to work in the industry. This all helped to bring a social transformation and new hope into the area. The fact that this hope was the result of a church initiative also softened people's hearts towards the gospel. They could see love in action which was transforming their lives and communities.

Bishop John's foresight in transferring the diocesan headquarters from the fairly remote area of Shyira Hill into the town of Musanze meant that as the country recovered and the tourist industry began to reassert itself once again, the Church could have a role in offering hospitality.

There are very few natural resources in Rwanda and the country is not much larger than Wales, but far more densely populated. In fact, Rwanda is the most densely populated country in Africa, and in order to prosper needs to exploit the natural resource of being one of the most beautiful countries in the world. The tourist industry has always been of great importance as people have visited to see the lakes and the mountains, the wildlife and birds.

In the east of Rwanda lies the Akagera game park, but during the war it became overgrown and many animals were killed. It has taken years for the park to recover and become a real tourist attraction again. The Nyungwe Forest in the west of the country was not a safe place for visitors for a long time following the genocide, because the dense tropical forest is almost impenetrable and became a hiding place for the fleeing militia insurgents after the war had officially ended. However, the Volcanoes National Park in the Virunga Mountains in the north, always a very popular destination for tourists who wanted to see the mountain gorillas, did not suffer the same amount of devastation.

The Virunga Mountains are a range of six extinct and three active volcanoes which straddle the borders of Rwanda, Uganda and the Democratic Republic of Congo (DRC). The Volcanoes National Park was made known to people in Europe and America by the work of the American primatologist, Dian Fossey. For twenty years she monitored the dwindling mountain gorilla population and worked tirelessly for their protection and survival. She became a household name after writing a book from which the film *Gorillas in the Mist* was made and released. Dian paid the ultimate price for protecting the gorilla population when she was brutally murdered in the mountains. Her murder was most likely the work of a poacher, but the mystery remains unsolved to this day. Her untimely death, however, stimulated even more interest in the mountain gorillas, and as soon as it was safe to return to Rwanda, there were people wanting to make a trek to visit them.

Fortunately the numbers of gorillas did not appear to decline too much through the war, and since then the government has had a vigorous policy of protection in place. They remain on the endangered species list, and the Virunga Mountains are one of the few places remaining where they can be seen in their natural environment.

The tourist lodges had been closed for safety reasons in 1994 and although they reopened for a short while in 1995, it was still too dangerous for visiting tourists, so they were closed again until 1999. Since the park reopened, the number of tourists visiting has constantly increased. In addition to the gorillas several other species of wildlife still roam the Virunga forests, and there have been 180 species of birds recorded. As well as the ever popular gorilla treks, tourists can also experience guided nature walks and mountain climbing. Musanze is the base for tourists who wish to visit the

Volcanoes National Park. In order to see the gorillas, the treks begin very early in the morning, so most visitors travel from Kigali the day before they are due to trek. This means that good accommodation to care for the tourists is an important part of the industry.

Bishop John supported this industry by building a church guest house on ground adjacent to the cathedral in Musanze. This not only offered safe accommodation and good food for travellers, but also there was room on the lawn in front of the complex for groups to camp, which made a cheaper option, especially for groups of young people. The Grace Guest House was not just for tourists, of course, but was able to host visitors who came to the diocese for all sorts of reasons and from all sorts of countries around the world. The rooms in Grace Guest House all have a small outside lounge which opens on to a garden courtyard. The guest house also has a swimming pool, the only one in Musanze.

The success of the guest house was such that it grew greatly in popularity and was often fully booked. It was this that made Bishop John realise that he could build a much larger complex, accommodating many more guests and with facilities for conferences and functions. So the dream of Ishema Hotel* was born. *Ishema* in Kinyarwanda means 'a feeling of deep pride in your achievement'. It was not that John had a deep pride in his own achievement, but that everyone working in the hotel would have pride in its quality of provision and service to all the guests.

The Ishema Hotel is a very well-appointed facility with 42 rooms, all with magnificent views of the mountains. All rooms have their own bathrooms and private balconies and are equipped with televisions and internet facilities.

The hotel also has four 'corner suites' which are more luxurious, having a sitting room as well as bedroom, and larger bathrooms. There are also two executive suites. These penthouse suites include

---

* See figure 005, page 155

an en suite master bedroom, a smaller bedroom and bathroom with separate shower and Jacuzzi, and a lounge / meeting room, and as such are used by important government officials from time to time when they come to Musanze for meetings.

The hotel and guest house are able to accommodate a total of 280 people for functions and the main conference room can seat 160 people. There is a full catering service, which can also cater for outside functions. There is a business centre to cater for conference clients, providing them with projectors and internet access, printing and copying services.

For weddings, the staff undertakes to do all the decorations for the reception, including the floral arrangements.

Even babysitting services are provided if required! There has been so much thought and planning to make Ishema Hotel a wonderful facility, providing for the needs of tourists, businessmen and conferences as well as local people who want to celebrate special life events in beautiful surroundings.

Bishop John's vision in building the hotel has meant that not only is the Church supporting the country's very important tourist trade, but it also supports local commerce with the facilities it provides. Ishema Hotel is one of the major employers in Musanze and provides a constant salary for many of the church members. Profits can be ploughed back into other projects to help the needy and spread the gospel. It hopes always to maintain standards that will be honouring to our Lord and Saviour.

Even though John has retired and no longer has responsibility for the hotel and guest house, he still has a vision to build yet another facility on the shore of Lake Burera! One day he drove me out to see the lovely lake and the beautiful countryside around.

"It would be a wonderful project, when I have the funds, to build a guest house here," Bishop John told me, showing me a tract of land which he bought a long time ago. The area is near the village where he grew up, and the lake was where he learnt to swim.

"It is so peaceful and would be a wonderful place for people to come for a retreat and renewal," he continued to tell me.

I had to agree! With the lake and the mountains, and lovely countryside all around, it would be a wonderful place to spend time away from the hustle and bustle of the town and have time to pray and meditate. I look forward to returning one day and staying there!

Chapter Twenty-One

HOPE GROWS THROUGH THE PEACEFUL YEARS

The Anglican diocese of Shyira had been founded on January 20th 1984. It was the third diocese to be formed, the others being Kigali and Butare. The diocesan boundaries covered a very large area and even after the formation of several other dioceses as the years passed and the Anglican Church grew in strength, Shyira still remained one of the largest.

When the diocese was first formed, a small Cathedral Church was built at Shyira, near the site of the original mission station. It began with just ten parishes and one secondary school.

After Bishop John was consecrated in 1997 he felt it would be better to have the focus of the diocese in Musanze, which was a good-sized town, a far more central location and served by a tarmac road from the capital, Kigali. Musanze was also the centre of the tourism trade, and as we have seen in the previous chapter, John was mindful of this as he planned the move from Shyira.

With the accent on evangelism and preaching the truth of the gospel, the number of new churches and parishes was growing. It became evident that there was a growing need for a new cathedral suitable for the twenty-first century. With all his usual enthusiasm and vision for the future Bishop John set about organising the blueprints, raising funds and starting construction. It had to be large enough to serve the Church, which was now growing by leaps and bounds. In 2004, St. John the Baptist Cathedral* was dedicated. It has the capacity to seat two thousand worshippers and is a light, airy, well-equipped building, with modern comfortable seating, a PA system, and a suite of offices for use by the bishop and diocesan officers. Although it is large, it retains a very real sense of the presence of God within the walls. It is beautiful in its simplicity and a wonderful legacy to leave for future generations.

The Church, however, is not the building! No-one knew better than Bishop John that the Church is the Body of Christ, the believers. The people in his diocese needed first to be evangelised and come to a saving faith in Christ and then to be built up in him. During his time as Bishop, John organised three major crusades, international in attendance. People came from Uganda, Australia, America, Burundi, Congo and Europe as well as from his own diocese. It took a huge amount of organisation to look after the hundreds of people who participated. They needed shelter and food as well as Bible teaching. All the hard work was amply rewarded, for many, many people accepted Jesus Christ as their Lord and Saviour at these crusade meetings!

Each archdeaconry also held their own missions and crusades in many of their parishes. In the years following the genocide many thousands of people who had previously only held a nominal Christian faith came to new birth in Jesus. This rapid church growth meant that a discipleship plan was needed. These 'babies' in Christ needed to be taught the Word of God and to grow into mature Christians who would live faithful lives and then go on to "teach others also" as Paul urges Timothy (in 2 Timothy 2:2, KJV) If the Church was to continue to grow and prosper in Shyira Diocese then Bishop John needed a programme to teach and train others so that

---

* See figure 002, page 154

they could disciple these new believers. With this in mind and in partnership with an organisation called Hope Rwanda, of which he was also the elected president, a large convention was organised to provide the training needed. It was held in the National Stadium in Kigali. Joyce Meyer came from America to be the guest speaker and Darlene Zschech was the worship leader for the convention. The stadium was packed for both days of meetings. This, again, was a very successful event and resulted in a good discipleship programme being introduced at the parish level. Bishop John trained up 250 of the believers to disciple others in their faith and to give Bible teaching back in their home communities and churches.

When Bishop John was nearing the Anglican Church's retirement age of sixty-five, although he still had plenty of energy to continue in office, he felt it right to stand down. He said, speaking to the Rwandan press: "What is important is not finishing what you started, but what foundation you laid for others."

This is typical of the humility of this man of God. For him, the importance was to lay a good foundation on which others could build, rather than being remembered for the works he had completed or success in the numbers of new believers which were achieved during his time in office.

One of the last forward-looking achievements Bishop John attained was to address the problem of how such a large diocese could be more effectively managed. His solution was to give half of it away.

In December 2008 the Shyira Diocese was divided in two. A new diocese for Gisenyi and Kibuye (now these towns have been renamed Rubavu and Kanongi, respectively) was formed, to the west of the region. It is called Kivu Diocese. A bishop was elected to serve this new diocese, and the large parish church in Gisenyi became the cathedral until such time as a new building could be erected. Gisenyi was once a holiday resort in the colonial times and still has a luxury hotel, Serena Kivu, but now is better known as the border town with

Congo. In fact, to me, it always seems 'half' a town, the other half being Goma, DRC. Through these troubled years the border has seen the exodus from Congo of many refugees, and the Church has a large mission to show love and hospitality to these poor people. It is good that there is a new diocese to care for them.

By the time Bishop John retired in 2010, the smaller Shyira Diocese had still grown to six archdeaconries, forty-seven parishes, the Cathedral chapter, and over three hundred local churches with 127,000 members.

There were also now fifty-two Anglican schools, thirteen of which taught to secondary level.

When Rt. Rev. Dr. Laurent Mbanda was consecrated as the third presiding Bishop of Shyira in March 2010, he inherited a thriving church, grounded in the Word of God, seeking to continue to proclaim the good news of Jesus to this part of the northern province of Rwanda.

I am reminded of something George Bernard Shaw wrote: "Life is no brief candle to me. It is a sort of splendid torch which I get to hold for a moment, and I want to make it burn as brightly as possible before turning it over to future generations."

A testimony to the 'turning over to future generations' was sent to Bishop John in February 2013 by a former pupil of Sonrise School. It reads:

Dear Bishop John,

I am grateful that you have [been] allowed to help us build our manhood until now. I am always delighted whenever I am see-ing the progress that I am making due to your struggle to found Sonrise, a home for the homeless, and because of the fact that you allowed [yourself] to carry the burden of being father to the fatherless orphans of which I am one. I don't ever forget the word you told us, that we have to keep our 'DIGNITY'. It built me and up to now. I thank you time and again. May God give you His love forever.

Attached is the propose [proposal] for the organisation Kevis and I have started. It is called 'UPLIFT RWANDA'. In this document you will be able to get the overview of our organisation. You will get its background and object[-ives] and what we intend to achieve.

In case I need to elaborate more, I will be glad to. I thank you again.

Your son,

Richard Ndekezi

The baton of love has been passed on to this young orphan who attended Sonrise. Richard and his colleague have now founded another organisation which will bring hope to their own people. They have been inspired by the example of Bishop John. I am sure this testimony will be repeated by many other young people who have been influenced, loved and cared for by John and Harriet. They have brought Jesus, the Hope of the nations, into their lives.

Chapter Twenty-Two

HOPE IN RETIREMENT

Love ever stands
With open hands,
And while it stands it lives,
forgives,
outlives.
And while it lives
It gives, and gives and gives.

(source unknown)

It has been stated within Christian circles that there is no such thing as retirement, only re-tyre-ment! This is certainly true for Bishop John and Harriet. It seems as if they have a new set of tyres and are back on the road of love even more powerfully than before! The little poem quoted above seems to fit their lives perfectly. Their lives are devoted to giving love and hope to others.

Since retirement in 2011 they have set up 'The Bishop John and Harriet Rucyahana Ministries', also known as 'Transformational Ministries'. This is a project to provide educational support to orphans and vulnerable children. John and Harriet have a vision to see Rwanda changed through better education – to see people believing in the hope of a better future.

Therefore they are committed to confronting the problems of Rwanda by helping to implement the 'Rwandan Vision 2020 – Excellency of Education and Purposed Teaching Core Values' (Rwandan Government Vision).

A research project in Rwanda conducted by Corine Siaens, K. Subbarao and Queentin Wodon in 2003 revealed that being an orphan is associated with a lower probability of school enrollment. The overall school attendance figures for Rwanda are: 76.4% of boys and 72.8% of girls attend school in urban areas, and 67.7% of boys and 67.7% of girls in rural areas.

In the case of orphans the numbers drop in urban areas to: boys 62.7% and girls 55.8%, and in rural areas to: 61.5% for boys and 62% for girls. To whom can these children turn for help and support to enable them to attend school?

It was to give such help that John and Harriet set up their ministry project. They want to alleviate the cycle of poverty which prevents children who want to get a good education from attending school by finding sponsors to help. Such people would provide the everyday materials which are needed for school life: uniforms, pens and pencils, exercise books, and a school bag – things which very poor parents or guardians are unable to provide for the children.

Bishop John and Harriet have set out three main objectives:

1. Assist orphans and vulnerable children through education facilities and psychosocial support. The programme will assist orphans and vulnerable children living within households in extreme poverty to move out of poverty by providing support to complete at least primary school, and in the case of orphans in households in extreme poverty, to also complete secondary school.

2. Inspire orphans and vulnerable children to become a good citizen through character training, Gospel fellowship, and counselling sessions for good academic performance.

3. Promote the wellbeing of orphans and vulnerable children through outreach programmes in order to deeply understand and respond to their concerns.

Bishop John and Harriet have made a statement of belief to back up the objectives of their ministry:

- Providing education to orphans and vulnerable children is a great contribution to breaking the cycle of intergenerational poverty.
- Poor access to education is central to lack of realisation of other human rights such as freedom of expression.
- Though primary education is free, many direct and indirect costs of schooling still have to be covered by parents and individual households, and inadequate funds for buying school materials remains a serious problem for some families living in poverty.
- Other limiting factors may become a barrier to orphans and vulnerable children to access primary education, including hunger, trauma, stigma and discrimination.

Bishop John and Harriet have set themselves some goals for the new ministry. These goals are wider than just helping to educate the children. They aim to develop Christian-based leadership qualities in the young people with whom they work, and to facilitate peace building, healing, reconciliation and transformation by: preaching Jesus Christ as Saviour; promoting research on issues facing Rwandans in the Great Lakes region; helping to strengthen and build institutional capacity based on moral values and respect for human rights; and improving the psychosocial and economic life of Rwandans through education and community-based dialogues. Through their teaching and ministry they pray they will reach and influence the communities of the whole of the Great Lakes area of Africa.

These are huge ambitions for a couple to take on in their retirement. However, all John's experience from the day when he began to teach the refugee children in the camps in Uganda until his retirement as Bishop of Shyira has taught him how much God can redeem in the lives of these disadvantaged children. God does have plans to give them a hope and a future!

John quotes from Isaiah 6:8, "'Whom shall I send? And who will go for us?' And I said, 'Here am I. Send me!'" God in His almighty wisdom has chosen ordinary people to do extraordinary things for Him! He needs us to be willing to help Him in His plans, and these include bringing hope and a future to those who are trapped in the pit of poverty.

One group of very disadvantaged children in Rwanda is the Batwa children. The Batwa are the smallest ethnic group and are related to the Congolese pygmy peoples. It is thought that there are around 34,000 people in a country which has a population of approximately eleven million. Historically these people have been marginalised and stigmatised, much as the gypsy people have been in Europe. It is part of the National Integration Plan that the problem of these children is addressed. Bishop John and Harriet have hearts which long to see these children have hope for a better future. As funds become available they want to help more of them. Although free education is now available for all children, the school drop-out rate from this community is high, partly because of the difficulty that families experience in funding the uniform and other school necessities, and partly because of the stigma such children face in school.

There are some BaTwa communities living in the foothills of the volcanoes in the Musanze district. They live in abject poverty, usually in a two-roomed mud-brick house with no running water or electricity. It is cold in the mountain area, especially at night, and most of these families have no beds, but sleep on a mattress (at the best) or a piece of sacking (at the worst) on the uneven mud floor with maybe just an old blanket to cover them. Open wood fires burn on the floors of the home, emitting dangerous fumes into the room where there are no windows. The fires also constitute a danger, especially to small children who have been known to roll over into the embers and suffer burns. Even the animals are often kept in the rooms, partly to protect them from theft. There is a feeling of lethargy and desperation within these communities, because they have no hope of change. It is tragic to think that such communities live within the shadow of the volcanoes where tourists pay hundreds of dollars to visit the lowland mountain gorillas! Such poor people live so near to the luxury tourist hotels!

The Bishop John and Harriet Rucyahana Transformational Ministries are based in a bungalow in Musanze, and along with a dedicated small staff, they work towards achieving their goals. One of their present short-term goals is to purchase a small tent to erect in the back garden of the office, so that they can hold training days for the children. I am sure these will be fun days, too, as well as times of learning!

Another urgent need, now that the ministry is effectively set up and running well, is to open an office in Kigali. The work is being partnered by Dave Ormesher and Global Livingstone Institution, and as it expands and broadens it will need this office in the capital, and also it is planned to open an office and have a supporting Board in the USA.

Bishop John's experience, learnt in Hoima and then so widely used both in Uganda and Rwanda as regards leadership development and evangelism training, will play a major part in the new Ministry he and Harriet have started.

John is convinced that it is essential to train leaders in Biblical principles. Vision for the nation and strategies for achieving goals and objectives must be well thought out, documented, implemented and evaluated. John states that it is vital that leaders possess a Biblically based character and ethics in order to avoid corruption and failure. The ministry therefore will plan and implement seminars and workshops that will focus on the inner, spiritual growth of leaders in the Church, politics, business and community. There will always be an emphasis on training youth leaders.

Bishop John received a letter from a young man, Christian Kayiteshonga, very recently. With permission from both parties concerned, I am including it as a testimony to Bishop John's commitment to training leaders.

Hello Daddy,

How are you doing? I hope you are well. I have been thinking so much lately and wondering why and how I have gotten to be who I am. And you kept appearing in my thoughts because of how much I have learned from you. I have learned to be a leader, an entrepreneur and a respective man from you.

I would like to take this opportunity and thank you so much for each and everything you ever taught me, and I am also grateful that I am still learning so much from you.

I thank God to have put you in my life because you have really been a blessing to me. I hope everything is going great for you, family and work.

I pray for you every day.

God bless you.
Thank you very much,
Christian Kayiteshonga

Christian first met Bishop John in 2000, when he was just a boy. His parents had known John for some time, but in 2000 he came to visit them and told them all about Sonrise School. They were so thrilled with all they heard that they decided to enrol their son, Christian. Christian says his first impression of Bishop John was that he appeared to be a great man full of wisdom and had a willingness to share that wisdom with others.

When Christian arrived at Sonrise School he found it a surprising place. Coming from a middle-class home, he had never before encountered so many poor children, many of them orphans.

He felt challenged by their good attitudes and wanted to learn more about their backgrounds and secrets of happiness. Rather than ever feeling superior because of the advantages with which he had been blessed, he felt humbled by these lovely students and many of them became his very best friends. He felt his world was enriched and enlarged by living with them at school, and knows this would never have happened without Bishop John.

He comments that the bishop taught him about taking responsibility and humble leadership. This helped him to grow into a confident young man. He learnt from Bishop John the need to be a job creator and not just a job seeker. Now he has been able to create his own non-profit-making company, called SekaRwanda, and graciously Bishop John agreed to become the chairman of the board, and in so doing is still helping and guiding this young man in his leadership role. *Seka* means 'smile' in Kinyarwanda and this service organisation started by Christian, along with a few other young professional friends, seeks to help the most needy in their society, bringing a smile to their faces. They are a new organisation, but have managed to take a supply of toothbrushes into two very poor villages and give them away to vulnerable children and widows. Something of Bishop John's love has rubbed off onto this young man, so that he can take the baton and run for his generation.

Throughout his Christian life Bishop John has acknowledged the calling and gifting of an evangelist, organising and preaching in many crusade meetings as well as training others to preach the gospel of Jesus Christ. He plans through the Ministry to continue to train others to evangelise; promote healthy theological discussion; hold crusades; continue preaching in the prisons; continue to help in the work of reconciliation; develop literature and other resources for leaders to use; hold conferences for both adult and youth leaders and hold retreats for pastors and Christian leaders. This ministry will focus on, but not be exclusive to, the Great Lakes region of Africa, which includes Burundi, Uganda, Congo, Tanzania, Rwanda and Kenya.

John and Harriet's Ministry is also committed to the economic and social transformation of African society. Key to those areas of development are the issues of reconciliation and justice, education, health and the elimination of poverty.

Since John and Harriet began this work in 2011 they have already held two conferences to train youth leaders in Musanze and held two other conferences for young people. Three students have been sponsored at senior school and university as well as children helped in primary school.

I have no doubt that many, many people will be blessed through John and Harriet's retirement ministry.

BIBLIOGRAPHY

Anyidoho, Henry Kwami. *Guns over Kigali*. Kampala, Uganda: Fountain Publishers, 1998.

Barnum, Thaddeus. *Never Silent*. Colorado Springs: Eleison, 2008.

Belinda, Lesley. *Colour of Darkness*. London: Hodder & Stoughton, 1996.

Belinda, Lesley. *With What Remains*. London: Hodder & Stoughton, 2006.

Briggs, Philip and Janice Booth. *Bradt Guide to Rwanda*. Bradt Travel Guides, 2004.

Carr, Rosamond Halsey and Ann Howard Halsey. *Land of a Thousand Hills*. New York: Plume Books (Penguin Group), 2000.

Church, J.F. *Quest for the Highest*. London: Paternoster, 1981.

Courtemanche, Gil. *A Sunday at the Pool in Kigali*. Edinburgh: Canongate, 2004.

Dallaire, Romeo. *Shake Hands with the Devil: The Failure of Humanity in Rwanda*. London: Arrow Books, 2004.

Ford, Margaret. *Janani: The Making of a Martyr*. London: Marshall, Morgan and Scott, 1978.

Gashumba, Frida. *Frida: Chosen to Die, Destined to Live.* Lancaster: Sovereign World, 2007.

Gatwa, Tharcisse. *The Churches and Ethnic Ideology in the Rwandan Crisis 1900–1994.* Milton Keynes: Paternoster, 2004.

Gourevitch, Philip. *We Wish to Inform You That Tomorrow We Will Be Killed with Our Families.* New York: Picador, 1998.

Guillebaud, Meg. *Service above All: History of Shyogwe as a Microcosm of the Country of Rwanda from 1946–2007.* Self-published, 1969.

Guillebaud, Meg. *Rwanda: The Land God Forgot?* Oxford: Monarch, 2002.

Guillebaud, Meg. *After the Locusts.* Oxford: Monarch, 2005.

Hatzfeld, Jean. *A Time for Machetes.* London: Serpent's Tail, 2003.

Ilibagiz, Immaculee. *Left to Tell.* Hay House, 2006.

Jansen, Hanna. *Over a Thousand Hills I Walk with You.* London: Andersen Press, 2008.

Kamukama, Dixon. *Rwanda Conflict.* Kampala, Uganda: Fountain Publishers, 1997.

Keane, Fergal. *Season of Blood.* London: Penguin, 1995.

Kehrer, Brigette. *Rwanda: Work of God, Work of Evil.* Destinee SA, 2002. www.destinee.ch

Kolini, Emmanuel M. and Peter R. Holmes. *Christ Walks Where Evil Reigned: Responding to the Rwandan Genocide.* Colorado Springs: Authentic, 2008.

Kyemba, Henry. *State of Blood.* London: Corgi Books, 1977.

Larson, Catherine Claire. *As We Forgive.* Grand Rapids: Zondervan, 2008.

Makower, Katharine. *Not a Gap Year but a Lifetime.* Eastbourne: Apologia Publications, 2008.

Miles, John. *Rwanda Rising from the Ashes.* Worthing: Verite CM Limited, 2011.

Millard, Mary Weeks. *After Genocide – There Is Hope*. UK: Terra Nova Publications, 2007.

Millard, Mary Weeks. *Emmanuel Kolini: The Unlikely Archbishop of Rwanda*. Colorado Springs: Authentic, 2008.

Misago, Celestin Kanimba and Thierry Mesas. *Regards sur le Rwanda*. Paris: Maison Neuve & Larose, 2003.

Oosterom, Wiljo Woodi. *Stars of Rwanda*. Amsterdam: Silent Work Foundation, 2004.

Osborn, H.H. *Fire in the Hills*. UK: Highland Books, 1991 (out of print).

Rucyahana, John and James Riordan. *The Bishop of Rwanda*. Nashville: Thomas Nelson, 2006.

Rusimbi, John. *The Hyena's Wedding*. London: Janus, 2007.

Sempangi, Kefa. *Reign of Terror, Reign of Love*. Tring, UK: Aslan/Lion Regal Books, 1979.

Ward, Kevin. *A History of Global Anglicanism*. Cambridge: Cambridge University Press, 2006.

Wooding, Dan and Ray Barnett. *Uganda Holocaust*. Grand Rapids: Zondervan / Glasgow: Pickering & Inglis, 1980.

APPENDIX 1

2011 World Convocation of Prison Fellowship International,
Sheraton Centre Hotel,
Toronto, Canada

26 June – 2 July 2011

The theme of the Jubilee Conference: Hope, Forgiveness, Freedom,
Restoration
Paper presented by Bishop John Rucyahana of Rwanda

Luke 4:18–19 (NIV)
"The Spirit of the Lord is on me, because he has anointed me to preach good news to the poor. He has sent me to proclaim freedom for the prisoners and recovery of sight for the blind, to release the oppressed, to proclaim the year of the Lord's favour."

The Scriptures are very transformational and life-giving for those in faith, and take courage to engage them. The Spirit of God who was in and upon Jesus was promised to us and given to us through Jesus, but we need to engage not only in faith but in obedience and surrender.

Allow me to use Rwanda as a case study or an example. Rwanda took it that Unity and Reconciliation was imperative; so much so as a foundation of our national restoration. To do that after decades of hatred and the genocide was not only hard but according to the flesh it was impossible.

- In order to get the Rwandans to realise their hope they had to be engaged and had to be obedient to the divine requirements, which are repentance with confession in truth, forgiveness with honesty in truth, then reconciliation and unity for Rwandan people followed. But it all began with hope.
- Hope gives energy and power to engage principles and policies that restore sanity, human dignity and development. People take responsibility for the past mistakes and history. We can't do much to change the Rwandan history, although we are responsible for it. At the same time we have all the promises from God to do better and have all the best future and development. Today we have reconciliation villages, survivors live with perpetrators of the genocide who have repented and were forgiven. Not only that, the country has engaged its hope for a better nation; people are producing and working together for national development.

It is never too late for God to save.

Esther 4:13–14 (NIV)

Mordecai's answer to Esther: "Do not think that because you are in the king's house you alone of all the Jews will escape. For if you remain silent at this time, relief and deliverance for the Jews will arise from another place, but you and your father's family will perish. And who knows but that you have come to royal position for such a time as this?" Mordecai said to Esther after Haman's conspiracy.

It is never too late to save and redeem the societies we belong to. We only need to let the healing, liberating, releasing Spirit of God come upon us and in us for His glory and for the sake of the people He intends to save.

Restorative Justice

Rwandan Gacaca courts (American jury is a lot like Gacaca):

a. Transparency
b. Credible source of evidence
c. Capable of handling the bulk of cases
d. Community participation
e. Trial took place where crimes were committed
f. Witnesses were in place

The traditional Gacaca is meant to truthfully expose and condemn the crime in order to redeem the repentant criminal.

God releases the prisoners from guilt and shame. God also released them from the prison cells as well, to the community service, and then from such to their homes.

Gacaca is therefore one of the ways of unity and reconciliation, because it provides room for the community consultations, participation, and together people find solutions for their common problems.

Reconciliation Barometer
(Research)

- 78.5% have experienced reconciliation and healing from the past
- 85.4% have experienced reconciliation personally
- 82.9% of the genocide perpetrators have demonstrated sufficient remorse
- 80.4% of Rwandans were convinced that most wrongdoers sought forgiveness since the genocide.

God uses leaders and gives to them vision and wisdom to carry out his redemptive mission. We thank God for the leadership of Rwanda who established an imperative unity and reconciliation policy for Rwandan people as the key to their restoration.

This is divine, based on the fact that Rwanda desired salvation and transformation, and made it a community mission. The recovery of Rwanda is by the hand of God. It is actually no less of a miracle like that of Susa in Esther's time.

Prison Fellowship Rwanda has contributed greatly in the restoration of the nation:

- The Umuvumu tree project has reached many hearts of prisoners. 45,000 were restored through conviction and repentance and then asked for forgiveness.
- The perpetrators who repented contributed immensely to Gacaca courts because they spoke the truth.
- Reconciliation results are witnessed and lived in the reconciliation villages and in the country at large.

Prison Fellowship's call, like that of other Christian ministries, is to engage the power of God in the Spirit, for the liberation of those God sends us to serve, the deprived (as a result of sin, social disorders such as bad leadership or otherwise).

I believe strongly that our call is not only to the inmates, but their families and the families of those whose lives were hurt by the inmates as well. Actually we are meant to reach our communities for Christ.

As 2 Corinthians 5:20 instructs us: We are Christ's ambassadors. God is pleading through us; we implore you on behalf of Christ to be reconciled to God and then to your neighbours.

Only 17 years since the genocide Rwanda is ranked by the World Bank and IMF as following:

- Rwanda being the least corrupt country in Africa
- Rwanda being the fastest-growing economy
- Rwanda being the best-governed state in Africa
- Rwanda being the cleanest state in Africa

- Rwanda being the best on how to do business in Africa
- Rwanda being the most secure country in Africa
- Rwanda being the best gender-sensitive country in Africa; the first to have the highest number of women in decision-making positions.
- Rwanda raised 51% of its national budget from its resources.

These registered success required co-operative efforts; to achieve the above Rwanda needed all the people, and of course not just one ethnic group can achieve that; not even the government official could, without community co-operation, make it.

These indicators are reflective of the humility to seek God's will and grace for transformation.

Conclusion

The Spirit of God is upon me for a purpose to go on his behalf and in his power (Matthew 28:18–19).

God is releasing people from the enslavement of sin, which draws us into physical crimes, death and humiliation.

God is restoring human dignity for those who believe in truth that God can save them and restore their nations when they come to Him in humility and repentance, seeking redemption. Such are being saved and Rwanda is one of them.

If Rwandan people can be ranked the way it has by the WB and IMF and is able to recover from the genocide then this is proof that any other nation of the world can also do it.

Bishop John Rucyahana
President of Prison Fellowship Rwanda
President of National Unity and Reconciliation Commission

APPENDIX 2

Meditations and Bible Studies which can be used with the book

Chapter 1

Bishop John made a comment. "You know, God does things in our lives, leading us into situations with a divine intention. Even then, He was preparing me for leadership."

Read Jeremiah 29:11; Psalm 139.

Questions:

1. Do you think that God has preplanned the minutiae of our lives?
2. Do our choices count? Does God need our cooperation for His plans to be implemented?
3. If we make bad choices, do we lose God's best for our lives?

Chapter 2

Issues of racial tensions and divisions.

Read Isaiah 60:1–3; Romans 10:12; Galatians 3:28.

Questions:

1. How does God view people of different races?

2. Should our commitment to members of God's kingdom override any commitment to our human ethnic group or nation?

3. How do we *honestly* feel about immigration / refugees and asylum seekers / cultural differences / minority groups e.g. gypsies?

Chapter 3

John paid respect to his father even when his own life was endangered.
Read Exodus 20:12; Ephesians 6:1–3.

Discuss the practicalities of the 'extended family' as opposed to the 'nuclear family'.
Questions:

1. What can we learn from the African 'extended family' model?

2. How can we obey this commandment if we have come from an abusive or dysfunctional family?

3. How do we work this out if our parents are not Christian or are anti-Christian and oppose our faith?

Chapter 4

Reading from the book of Acts, John found hope in Jesus.
Read Acts 2:1–47.
Questions:

1. Was this message just for the Jews (v. 22), or for the whole world?

2. What does Peter say is necessary for salvation?

3. How did the lifestyle of the new believers change?

4. Do our churches reflect this kind of community?

Chapter 5

Marriage to Harriet.
Read Proverbs 31:10–31; Amos 3:3; Proverbs 12:4.

Questions:

1. What does Amos 3:3 mean in this day and age?
2. In choosing a life partner what should be the important things to consider?
3. In this age of high divorce rates how can we maintain and protect marriage?
4. Is the description of the wife in Proverbs 31 relevant in postmodern society?
5. What can she teach us?

Chapter 6

Helping disadvantaged people.
Read Matthew 25:31– 46.
Questions:

1. How relevant is this passage in the 21st century in the country in which we live?
2. What project might Jesus be asking us to start, or become involved with, in our own community?

The issue of studying.
Read 1 Timothy 4:7–8; 2 Timothy 2:15; 2 Timothy 3:14–17.
Questions:

1. How important is it for a Christian leader to study and undergo training?
2. Some Christians say that the Holy Spirit is the only teacher we need. What do you think about that statement?

Chapter 7

Issues of corruption in society.
Read Proverbs 11:1; Micah 2:1–2; Amos 4:1; 5:11–12; 8:4–7.
Questions:

1. What do you think these scriptures tell us about God?

145

2. Think about the recent news you have read/heard. Are there any examples of corruption?

3. How can we be salt and light in a corrupt society?

Chapter 8

The work of evangelists.

Read Matthew 28:18–20; Mark 1:14–18.

Questions:

1. Are these commands for twenty-first-century Christians or just for the time of the apostles?

2. How are we, as disciples, proclaiming the good news of Jesus in our community?

3. Can we think of new ways to reach people who have no interest in the gospel?

Chapter 9

The Mustard Seed Orphanage.

Read Exodus 22:21–23; Psalm 146:7–9; Isaiah 1:17; James 1:27.

Questions:

1. Why does God have such a heart for orphans and widows?

2. In the twenty-first century is there a need to obey these scriptures? Can these issues be left to the state to take care of?

3. How have needs changed through the centuries? Think of creative ways in which widows and orphans or single-parent families could be helped in the community where you live.

Chapter 10

Healing for grief.

Read Psalm 147:3; Psalm 145:8–9; Isaiah 49:14–16; 61:1–3; Lamentations 3:31–33.

Questions:

1. Can deep wounds such as people received in the genocide ever be healed?
2. Have you received God's comfort at any time? Can you share how this happened?

Chapter 11

Issues of repentance.
Read Jeremiah 15:19; Luke 3:7–8; 2 Corinthians 7:10.
Questions:

1. What does the Biblical word 'repentance' mean?
2. Can a person become a Christian without repentance?
3. Should repentance be a 'one off' or a continuing part of our lives?
4. Discuss why 'sorry' is the hardest word to say.

Chapter 12

Rebuilding a nation and rebuilding trust.
Read Isaiah 57:14–19; 58:6–12; 61:1–9.
Questions:

1. Where can a nation find hope after civil war and devastation?
2. What do these verses teach us concerning individual responsibility to help rebuild a nation?
3. How can we be peacemakers in our own community?

Chapter 13

Learning to live, love, and work together without prejudice.
Read Acts 10.
Questions:

1. What were Peter's prejudices which the Lord needed to address?

2. How can children be helped to accept each other?

3. What prejudices do you have? Which groups of people do you naturally shy away from?

4. Do you think God wants you to change this attitude and how might you address this problem?

Chapter 14

Examining agape love.

Read 1 Corinthians 13; Galatians 6:12; 1 Thessalonians 4:9.

Questions:

1. Are we like the Thessalonians, known for our love?

2. "Love always hopes" – How can we cultivate a spirit which sees and hopes for the best in others?

3. How can we put our love into action in our daily lives?

Chapter 15

Standing up for the truth of the gospel.

Read Luke 6:22–23; Ephesians 6:2–20; 2 Timothy 1:6–7; 2:1–7.

Questions:

1. Do you believe that the Bible has something to say about every issue we face?

2. How can we 'strengthen ourselves' to stand up for our convictions?

3. Jesus promised we would face opposition. Why can we rejoice when this happens?

Chapter 16

Issues of healing.

Questions:

1. Read Isaiah chapter 53 v. 4 & Matthew chapter 8 vs. 14–17
   Does Jesus' healing ministry still continue into the 21st century?
   Discuss any personal experience you may have of miraculous healing.

2. Read Matthew Chapter 9 vs. 27–31

   What part does faith play in healing ministry both in the life of the one seeking healing and also in the person ministering?

3. Read John chapter 5 v. 1–8.

   Consider verse 6.

   Why did Jesus ask this question? Is it possible to become too comfortable living with a disease to not really want to be healed?

4. Read John chapter 9 v. 1-34 (if time) and consider verses 1–3.

   Are we judgemental concerning people who may be sick from what we might consider 'self-inflicted' illness? E.g. disease caused by smoking, obesity, sexual promiscuity?

   Is sickness ever the result of sin?

   Do we have caring hearts for people who might have these sorts of conditions and love them as Jesus would?

5. Read 2 Corinthians 12 vs. 7–10

   Paul clearly had a medical problem from which he wasn't healed.

   What does this passage tell us about his attitude?

   How can we apply this today in the healing ministry of the Church?

Chapter 17

Issue of work ethic.
Read 2 Thessalonians 3:7–13.
Questions:

1. What should our attitude be to those who refuse to get a job? How can we help them?

2. How can we help unemployed people find meaningful occupation? Pray for any people you might know in this situation.

Issue of forgiveness.

Read Matthew 5:21–24; 6:5–15; James 5:6.

Questions:

1. Does Jesus really mean that He will not forgive us *unless* we forgive others?
2. What does unforgiveness do to our relationships?
3. How does forgiveness open the offender's heart?
4. How does forgiveness change the victim's heart?

Chapter 18

Issue: Working hard for the sake of the Gospel.

Read 1 Corinthians 3:5–15; 15:10; 2 Corinthians 12:9.

Questions:

1. How can we build with quality materials which will last?
2. Are we willing to be just a 'link in the chain' or do we need to be 'top dog'?

Chapter 19

Issue of giving up the right to revenge.

Read Matthew 5:43–48; Romans 12:14–21.

Questions:

1. It is easy to hold on to bitterness and the right to revenge. Why should we give it up?
2. How will these attitudes affect our lives in the long term if we decide to hold on to them?
3. Who benefits most, the perpetrator or the victim, if the right of revenge is given back to God?
4. Can we trust God to deal fairly with the person who has hurt us?

Chapter 20

Issue of service to your country.
Read Matthew 17:24–27; 22:15–22; Romans 13:1–7; 1 Timothy 2:1–4; 1 Peter 2:13–17.
Questions:

1. Does our earthly citizenship matter to God?
2. Are there times when our loyalty to God must supersede our loyalty to our country?
3. How might our Christian principles make us model citizens?

Chapter 21

Issues of responsibility in our community.
Questions:

1. Can just one person make a difference in his/her community/country?
2. Have we got the vision to see what needs to be tackled and the faith to take action?
3. What are the major poverty issues your community faces? Pray about what God might be calling you to do to change things.

Chapter 22

Issue of retirement years.
Read Psalms 92:12–15; 103:1–5; Isaiah 46:4.
Questions:

1. Is there any retirement for a Christian?
2. Many people fear old age – what should the Christian's attitude be to this stage of life?
3. How can you support older people and encourage them in ministry, especially if their strength is failing?

APPENDIX 3: PHOTOGRAPHS

Figure 1 A view of the majestic Virunga Volcanoes – home to the lowland mountain gorillas.

Figure 2 The Cathedral at Ruhengeri / Musanze which replaced the old cathedral for the Shyira Diocese.

Figure 3 The Rwandan flag proudly flying at Sonrise Senior School.

Figure 4 Bishop John and his wife, Harriet.

Figure 5 Ishema Hotel in Ruhengeri / Musanze – an income generating project for the diocese.

Figure 6 Victims and perpertrators of genocide now living and working together in the reconciliation village.

Figure 7 Bishop John Rucyahana wearing a kanzu – the traditional robe worn by Ugandan men.

Lightning Source UK Ltd.
Milton Keynes UK
UKOW06f0135120416

272056UK00001B/80/P